T0284855

My Mother, My Teacher:
A Memoir from Western Sahara

Jadiyetu Mint Omar Uld Ali Uld Embarek Fal, 1942–2006. Photo
provided by José María Rojo Vian (Chema), 2003.

BAHIA MAHMUD AWAH

My Mother, My Teacher:
A Memoir
from Western Sahara

EDITED AND TRANSLATED BY
Dorothy Odartey-Wellington

The Modern Language Association of America
New York   2024

© 2024 by The Modern Language Association of America
85 Broad Street, New York, New York 10004
www.mla.org

All rights reserved. MLA and the MODERN LANGUAGE ASSOCIATION
are trademarks owned by the Modern Language Association of America.
To request permission to reprint material from MLA book publications,
please inquire at permissions@mla.org.

To order MLA publications, visit www.mla.org/books. For wholesale and
international orders, see www.mla.org/bookstore-orders.

The MLA office is located on the island known as Mannahatta
(Manhattan) in Lenapehoking, the homeland of the Lenape people. The
MLA pays respect to the original stewards of this land and to the diverse
and vibrant Native communities that continue to thrive in New York City.

Cover illustration: *La abuela maestra*, by Aawah Walad.

Originally published as *La maestra que me enseñó en una tabla de madera*
(Sepha, 2011).

Texts and Translations 43
ISSN 1079-2538

Library of Congress Cataloging-in-Publication Data

Names: Mahmud Awah, Bahia, 1960- author. | Odartey-Wellington,
    Dorothy, 1964- editor, translator.
Title: My mother, my teacher : a memoir from Western Sahara / Bahia
    Mahmud Awah ; edited and translated by Dorothy Odartey-Wellington.
Other titles: Maestra que me enseñó en una tabla de madera. English
Description: New York : The Modern Language Association of America,
    2024.
Series: Texts and translations, 1079-2538 ; 43 | "Originally published as
    La maestra que me enseñó en una tabla de madera (Sepha, 2011)."—Title
    page verso. | Includes bibliographical references.
Identifiers: LCCN 2023050695 (print) | LCCN 2023050696 (ebook) |
    ISBN 9781603296458 (paperback) | ISBN 9781603296465 (EPUB)
Subjects: LCSH: Mahmud Awah, Bahia, 1960- | Mahmud Awah, Bahia,
    1960—Family. | Authors, North African—21st century—Biography. |
    Sahrawi (African people)—Biography. | Western Sahara—Biography. |
    BISAC: BIOGRAPHY & AUTOBIOGRAPHY / Personal Memoirs |
    BIOGRAPHY & AUTOBIOGRAPHY / Literary Figures | LCGFT:
    Autobiographies.
Classification: LCC PQ8619.M34 Z46 2024b (print) | LCC PQ8619.M34
    (ebook) | DDC 868/.6403 [B]—dc23/eng/20240117
LC record available at https://lccn.loc.gov/2023050695
LC ebook record available at https://lccn.loc.gov/2023050696

CONTENTS

INTRODUCTION:
LESSONS IN THE SAHARAWI
ART OF REMEMBERING

When a group of people are forced to flee from their homeland, they do so to preserve their lives. In their involuntary exodus, they are also driven by a desire to protect their way of being. As displaced people, they endeavor to retain a sense of continuity of place, practices, and relationships when they settle elsewhere, still with the hope of reclaiming their land. To retain their notion of who they are and where they have come from, however, they need to remember. As Jan Assmann puts it, "One has to remember in order to belong" (114). Bahia Mahmud Awah's memoir in honor of his mother, *Mi madre, mi maestra: Memorias del Sáhara Occidental (My Mother, My Teacher: A Memoir from Western Sahara)*,[1] offers lessons in the art of fulfilling that imperative. It provides an opportunity to reflect on how contemporary Saharawis who have been exiled from their homeland, Western Sahara, contribute to a sense of identity through memory. As one example of Hispano-Saharawi creative expression, *My Mother, My Teacher* illustrates the roles played by displacement, imagined memory, oral poetry, and gender in our understanding of the art of Saharawi memory making.

Hispano-Saharawi Creative Expression

Mahmud Awah is a founding member of the Generación de la Amistad Saharaui (Saharawi Generation of Friendship),[2] a group of exiled writers from Western Sahara, a former

Spanish colony, whose creative work is shaping the idea of contemporary Saharawi literature and culture. The Chilean poet Maribel Lacave describes the Saharawi Generation of Friendship as "un grupo de poetas saharauis, que tienen en común tres características principales: el compromiso intelectual y poético con la liberación de su pueblo, el uso del lenguaje escrito frente a la tradición oral de la poesía saharaui y el hecho de escribir su obra en español" ("a group of Saharawi poets who have three main characteristics in common: a poetic and intellectual commitment to the liberation of their people, the use of written language in the face of traditional Saharawi oral poetry, and the fact of writing in Spanish"; 20).

As a literary group, their growing corpus of works can be found in many online venues, most notably on the blog *Y . . . ¿dónde queda el Sáhara? (And . . . Where Exactly Is Western Sahara?*; blogs.elpais.com/donde-queda-el-sahara), and in various anthologies, including Mahmud Awah and Conchi Moya's *Don Quijote, el azri de la badia saharaui (Don Quixote, Knight-Errant of the Saharawi Nomad Lands)* and Mohamed Salem Abdelfatah's *Las voces del viento: Poesía saharaui contemporánea (Voices in the Wind: Contemporary Saharawi Poetry)*. However, according to the group's website, when they came together in 2005 ("III aniversario"), they had previously published, both individually and collectively, various works that already revealed their aesthetic projects as well as their common themes and concerns.[3] The echoes of loss, longing, identity, trauma, and other exilic issues in the abovementioned anthologies—and in works such as Mahmud Awah's *Versos refugiados (Refugee Poems)*, Limam Boisha's *Ritos de jaima (Jaima Rituals)*, Salem Abdelfatah's *La joven del pozo (The Girl at the Well)*, and Ali Salem Iselmu's *Un beduino en el Caribe (A Bedouin in the Caribbean)*—are all rooted in the recent history of Western Sahara.

Thanks to the work of the Generation of Friendship, and to Hispano-Saharawi creative expression in general, research interest in Western Sahara—hitherto dominated by social science disciplines—has expanded to include interest in the aesthetic dimension of the Saharawi quest for sovereignty and its related themes. Indeed, the diverse range of critical perspectives inspired by this growing body of creative work is evident in publications such as Alberto López Martín's "Cultural Resistance and Textual Emotionality in the Sahrawi Poetic Anthology *VerSahara*," Debra Faszer-McMahon's "Images of the Global Hispanophone: Transnational Iconography in Saharaui Literature," Joanna Allan's "Decolonizing Renewable Energy: Aeolian Aesthetics in the Poetry of Fatma Galia Mohammed Salem and Limam Boisha," and Mahan Ellison's "'La Amada Tiris, Tierra de Nuestros Abuelos': The Affective Space of the Sahara in Hispano-Saharawi Literature." Despite the burgeoning interest in Saharawi creative culture, there is a dearth of critical work on audiovisual representations of Saharawi identity, particularly on those audiovisual accounts by Saharawis themselves. Examples of the latter include *Leyuad: Un viaje al pozo de los versos* (*Leyuad: A Journey to the Well of Poetry*), codirected by Brahim Chagaf, Gonzalo Moure, and Inés G. Aparicio; *Legna: Habla el verso saharaui* (*Legna: Saharawi Poetry Speaks*), codirected by Mahmud Awah, Juan Robles, and Juan Carlos Gimeno; *Belgha, la memoria viva* (*Belgha, Living Memory*), directed by Man Chagaf; and the numerous short films directed by graduates of the Saharawi film school at the refugee camps, Escuela de Formación Audiovisual Abidin Kaid Saleh (Abidin Kaid Saleh Film School).[4]

Hispano-Saharawi creative expression is rooted in the recent history of Western Sahara, where efforts to rid the region of European colonization did not yield the outcome experienced by other Africans who fought for independence in the

1950s and 1960s. As happened with the only other former Spanish colony on the continent, Equatorial Guinea, Spain declared Western Sahara an overseas province of Spain in 1958 in order to buttress the Franco regime's claims to the United Nations that it did not possess any colonies at that time. However, while Equatorial Guinea gained independence from Spain in 1968, Western Sahara, which had become the target of the expansionist ambitions of its neighbors Morocco and Mauritania, was partitioned between the two countries through a tripartite agreement with Spain in 1975. The complex history and circumstances surrounding the derailment of Western Sahara's independence fall outside the ambit of this brief introduction. Readers may, however, turn to Enrique Bengochea Tirado and Francesco Correale for their discussion of the social and political transformation of the region in the latter decades of Spanish colonization in "Modernising Violence and Social Change in the Spanish Sahara, 1957–1975." Furthermore, expert analyses of the conflict itself can be found in such works as *Endgame in the Western Sahara: What Future for Africa's Last Colony?*, by Toby Shelley, and *Western Sahara: War, Nationalism, and Conflict Irresolution*, by Stephen Zunes and Jacob Mundy. Similarly, Samia Errazzouki and Allison L. McManus's *Beyond Dominant Narratives on the Western Sahara* and Raquel Ojeda-García and colleagues' *Global, Regional and Local Dimensions of Western Sahara's Protracted Decolonization: When a Conflict Gets Old* provide a multidisciplinary discussion not only of the conflict but also of its regional and global ramifications. In addition, Irene Fernández-Molina and Ojeda-García provide an update on the repercussions of the conflict in "Western Sahara as a Hybrid of a Parastate and a State-in-Exile: (Extra)Territoriality and the Small Print of Sovereignty in a Context of Frozen Conflict."

Rhetorics of Displacement

The Mauritanian and Moroccan occupation of Western Sahara and protracted war against the Polisario led to the displacement of many Saharawis.[5] Mahmud Awah's memoir gives readers a close-up look at one family's personal experience of loss, separation, and displacement in the aftermath of the failed decolonization process. At the beginning of the war, Mahmud Awah's family, along with other Saharawis, had to leave their town—Auserd—to seek refuge elsewhere. However, their place of refuge soon came under attack from Mauritanian soldiers, who rounded up and led off both young and older men, including Mahmud Awah's uncles and father. Thus, fearing for her son's safety, Mahmud Awah's mother asked her son to flee to a Polisario base in Gleybat Legleya, in the hope that he would be protected there. He was fifteen at the time. Mother and son would not see each other again for a decade. Mahmud Awah spent three of those years at a boarding school in Algeria.[6] He subsequently went on to Cuba with other Saharawi youth for his postsecondary education. Meanwhile, in 1979, his family joined other refugees who had settled in camps near Tindouf, Algeria, since the mass exodus in the mid-1970s. It was there—the refugee camps where today some 173,600 Saharawis live[7]—that Mahmud Awah's mother passed away in 2006, never having fulfilled her dream of returning to her homeland. Quite the contrary, she passed on far away from her native land, where one of her siblings still lives, and even farther away from her son, who had resettled in Spain. Saharawis, like Mahmud Awah's family, find themselves dispersed over at least four geographic spaces: the occupied Western Sahara, the parts of Western Sahara under Polisario control (known as the liberated territories), the refugee camps near Tindouf, and Spain.

The geographic fragmentation of Western Sahara is responsible for what can be described as "extraterritoriality" in the former Spanish colony's contemporary creative expression. I refer to literature by Mahmud Awah and the Generation of Friendship as extraterritorial writing for two reasons: first, it emerged outside the writers' territory and in digital spaces; second, its representations of identity echo with "rhetorics of displacement," to borrow Katrina Powell's term, which include "nostalgia, a particular sense of home, belonging, citizenry, and the right of return" (302). At the core of the Saharawi narrative of displacement is the bilingualism that is upheld by Mahmud Awah and the Generation of Friendship as an identity marker, a bilingualism that combines the mother tongue and the colonial language. Hassaniya, the traditional Saharawi language, and Spanish, acquired not only through colonization but also through pan-Hispanic alliances, are employed as distinct features that serve to reinstate the boundaries between Western Sahara and Morocco. Writing in Hassaniya, Spanish, or both—creating a distinctive Hispano-Saharawi form of expression—is an act of resistance to displacement. Therefore, this writing serves to symbolically return Saharawis to the territory from which they are exiled.

Rhetorics of displacement are also manifested in the authors' preoccupation with imaginings of home, a central feature of *My Mother, My Teacher*. In the absence of territory, rhetorical strategies for bridging the spatial and temporal gap between the writers and the space from which they have been displaced rely on memory. Memory is the impetus for other works by Mahmud Awah, such as his autobiographical *El sueño de volver* (*The Dream of Going Back*) and his aforementioned co-directed documentary on Saharawi oral poetry, *Legna: Habla el verso saharaui*. It also resonates in other Saharawi writing, including Boisha's *Los versos de madera* (*Poetry Etched in Wood*).

Furthermore, in reading *My Mother, My Teacher*, one gets the sense that Saharawis who fled Western Sahara metaphorically took with them to the Algerian *hammada*—an Arabic term for rocky, flat, desert terrain such as the area in which Saharawi refugees have settled near Tindouf in Algeria—or to Spain the life-giving energy of their land. It is therefore beneficial to draw on theories advanced in memory studies, as I do here, in the reading of this memoir.

Imagined Memory

According to Thomas Docherty, "[M]emory is central to the construction of a polity" (50). In other words, memory is fundamental to the creation of a cohesive community that is bound by a sense of shared identity. How then do displaced people, such as Saharawi refugees, some of whom may not have direct knowledge of the place they call home, participate in the process of constructing a national identity? How do Saharawis such as Mahmud Awah's mother, who experienced the exodus firsthand, transfer their recollections of the place that they have been forced to leave to those who were not part of the exodus? How are Saharawis who were born in exile supposed to find their way home? One may find answers to some of these questions in a reading of *My Mother, My Teacher* as an exemplar of what I refer to as "imagined memory."

The qualifier "imagined," as used here, derives from Benedict Anderson, who wrote that a nation "is *imagined* because the members of even the smallest nation will never know most of their fellow-members, meet them, or even hear of them, yet in the minds of each lives the image of their communion" (6). Similarly, the memory of home that is preserved by displaced people is imagined. It relies on narratives of traditions, values, knowledge, and legends that are timelessly recreated and shared by the community, regardless of the differences that may exist in the community's chronological and spatial proximity to that home and to the events surrounding the original departure from it. A sense of belonging is imagined through those narrative threads that are used to shape a place as the locus of one's identity with others, to paraphrase Docherty (54), as they are handed down from generation to generation. "Imagination" is what we call the evocation of a place in a person who has not experienced it firsthand, Docherty notes, and in that sense "memory and imagination are intertwined, . . . and their focal point, their intersection, is what we call our own identity" (55). Similar thoughts are echoed in the observation that "[p]eoples, nations, are constituted, made so . . . by a story, a Book of many chapters, populating our imaginations with memories common to all members" (Moseley 65).

Imagined memory is essential to populations who, for one reason or another, have lost access to the place that they call home. In her research on Australian Aboriginal people, Lynette Russell observed that "landscapes of the mind" were the means by which Aboriginal people, for example, bypassed colonial barriers to their "country" in order to pass it on to future generations (402). Furthermore, she added, those imagined places "represent real, viable and tangible links to their heritage" (402). The same appears to be true of contemporary Saharawis as represented in Mahmud Awah's work. *My Mother, My Teacher* reads like a window into the social, cultural, and aesthetic practices by which Saharawis pass on, to current and future generations, the territory to which they no longer have physical access. It is a model of transgenerational creation and communication and of the venues in which ideas of self and place are molded into portable form through poetry and story.

Although *My Mother, My Teacher* begins and ends with the life and death, respectively, of the author's mother, its various accounts do not follow a chronological order. The memoir's nonlinear structure may reflect the nature of human recall itself. However, it is also the result of the transgenerational mode of communication that is meant to point the way home, so to speak, in Saharawi culture. Most of the accounts in the work revolve around the author's mother, whom he calls "Detu." As the main remembering subject, Detu connects her generation to those that precede and follow it. Meanwhile, Mahmud Awah, as the narrative voice of the memoir, travels back and forth through time, retrieving and transmitting first-, second-, or thirdhand accounts. The resultant text is a set of polyphonic and fragmented stories that are held together by their transgenerational relevance. The section of the memoir titled "Las tertulias y el sabio Deylul" ("The Gatherings and Deylul, the Wise One") illustrates the above structure. Just like other sections of the work, it does not have a chronological or even thematic connection to the section preceding or immediately following it. However, it reflects a common feature of several memories in the work: it exemplifies the transgenerational transference of traditional knowledge, which is symbolized by Deylul, a fount of Indigenous information on the flora, fauna, and climate of the Sahara. By constantly referencing Deylul, Detu passes on the aforementioned wisdom to her interlocutors along with a symbolic ownership of the land, the source of that knowledge. The transgenerational communication in the memoir creates a sense of provenance and continuity where spatial and temporal distance would inspire sentiments of separation and loss.

The mode of social interaction in Saharawi culture facilitates the kind of transgenerational communication described above. In the memoir, we learn of the "tertulias" ("gatherings"), where family and friends congregate to converse leisurely—in both prose and verse—over several rounds of tea. The fact that these social gatherings are evoked numerous times in the memoir attests to their ubiquity in Saharawi social practice. Those venues in which Mahmud Awah heard his mother (and indeed other family members and friends) tell and retell the stories that shape Saharawi identity provide continuous "opportunities for and acts of shared remembering" (Erll, "Locating" 313). These regular acts of communal remembering give uniformity to the memories of home and render them familiar across time and space. Continuity occurs not only through the retelling of stories but also through the gatherings themselves. As social contexts in which identities are formed, the gatherings are essentially portable cultural spaces that can be reproduced wherever Saharawis find themselves.

In discussing the constructive nature of family memories, Astrid Erll notes that "memories are rarely rehearsed for their own sake" and that they "fulfil normative and formative, value-related and identity-related functions" ("Locating" 307). The family stories that are retrieved and retold in Mahmud Awah's memoir, and at the gatherings, are no exception. The story that Detu would tell her family of how her father almost starved to death in a windstorm is one such "normative and formative" account. It tells of the resilience not only of Mahmud Awah's grandfather Omar but also of his grandmother Nisha, who was left to calm the fears of her children and keep together the family's livestock in the absence of her husband. It resonates with the positive outcome of a symbiotic and respectful relationship between humans and nature. It also reflects the skills that enabled both Omar and Nisha to overcome the nature-driven challenges in their nomadic life. The fact that the knowledge behind these qualities derives from the specificity of the land suggests that they are traditional qualities and that the values that they represent are generically Saharawi and, consequently, replicable.

Memory shapes the image that a community has of itself through what is selected to be recorded in the community's oral tradition. Additionally, whatever is selected is determined by a prevailing context, which in Mahmud Awah's memoir is the recent history of the Saharawis. For Saharawis, Spanish colonization, the failed process of decolonization, Moroccan occupation, and life in exile in refugee camps all loom large in their acts of meaning making and identity construction. Consequently, much of contemporary Saharawi creative expression is informed by collective or personal experiences related to the above context and rests on an undercurrent of self-assertion and protest. For example, while celebrating Detu's acts of remembering, *My Mother, My Teacher* also speaks back to, and against, past and ongoing attempts to undermine Saharawi sovereignty. The author's recollection of one of the family stories about an uncle illustrates how family anecdotes record resistance to external acts of domination. On the surface, the story could simply be a humorous account of how Mahmud Awah's uncle Mohamed Moulud took down some flags that had been installed by the Spanish army just because they were invading his space and interfering with the freedom of his herd of camels. He made a *darraa*, the traditional Saharawi male outfit, for himself and reins for his camels with some of the flags and then set fire to the rest. Although Moulud's actions do not appear to be motivated by activism, their political symbolism is self-evident. That symbolism is reinforced by the year in which the story took place, 1956. Around that time, anti-colonial fervor was rife in the region: Morocco and Tunisia had gained independence that year, and the Algerian War of Independence was ongoing. Indeed, the Liberation Army under Benhamou Mesfioui had begun to organize an offensive against Spain in Western Sahara in January of that year (Pazzanita and Hodges xxviii).

Furthermore, Allal al-Fassi, a Moroccan nationalist leader, was by that time also making claims of a "Greater Morocco," a map of which appeared in his party's newspaper (Zunes and Mundy 36). All these circumstances help reimagine Moulud's personal act as an act of subversion against external forces of domination.

Oral Poetry

My Mother, My Teacher illustrates the notion that creative oral expression, a leitmotif in the memoir, serves as a signpost that points the way home in Saharawi culture. It echoes Mahmud Awah's assertion elsewhere that oral poetry is the repository of the history and the identity of a people ("Oral Literature" 62). Memory, poetry, geography, and identity intersect in one of Mahmud Awah's many conversations with his mother, in which she expresses her longing to be in a part of the Sahara that was behind the occupiers' walls—a system of walls, put in place by Morocco, between the occupied lands and the territory controlled by the Polisario—"[e]n la falda de Galb Ashalay" ("[o]n the slopes of Galb Ashalay"). The author's response to his mother's nostalgia—"Mamá, debes preguntar al poeta Badi, porque tiene un poema dedicado a Galb Ashalay" ("Mama, you've got to ask Badi the poet, because he has a poem dedicated to Galb Ashalay")—underscores the use of poetry to creatively place displaced Saharawis back onto their land. The art of defying displacement through poetry is itself an age-old skill employed by traditional Saharawi poets who found themselves far away from home. According to Mahmud Awah, Saharawi oral poetry draws on a nomadic tradition whereby the wandering poet would evoke the land that they had left behind, praising it over the one in which they found themselves ("Oral Literature" 62).

In other words, for nomadic Saharawis, poetry served to memorialize their past land and time.

Although the days of nomadic errancy are long gone, the abovementioned poetic tradition continues to be relevant because of the current situation of forced displacement. Mahmud Awah's mother, and other poets, continue to inscribe their poetry onto the landscape from which they have been expelled, as though to enable future generations to recognize it as their own. One such poem cited in this memoir is a *tebraa* that Detu composed to commemorate her reunion with her sister and other family members in the liberated region after thirty years of separation. *Tebraa* is a traditional poetic form in Hassaniya that is cultivated exclusively by women for a female audience. Traditionally, it dealt with themes related to love in an intimate setting.[8] In the poem, the imagery of a heart roaming unencumbered among the hills and the *jaimas*—portable nomadic dwellings—in the liberated territories is used to metaphorically break down the physical boundaries that have been imposed by exile and the occupation. Indeed, the recurrent poetic references to place of origin or belonging in *My Mother, My Teacher* function in the same way as would a flag or similar material emblem: as a record in verse that stands in for the person or persons who may be absent from that location. Additionally, in citing his mother's *tebraa*, Mahmud Awah contributes to preserving women's poetic memorialization of their land. This is significant, as his mother's compositions, like other *tebraa*, are susceptible to loss because of the conditions of long-term refugeehood.

Traditional poetry also makes it possible to hand down to generations of displaced Saharawis a seemingly concrete and enduring place to which they might return. In the memoir, Tiris, the land of Detu's birth and the region that she and her family had to abandon, is such a place. As a region of pasture-land in the nomadic tradition, it lends its image and imagery to the creation of a mythical place of plenty, well-being, and refuge that contrasts with the occupied territory as well as the infertile Algerian *hammada* where Saharawis live in exile. Indeed, in a work devoted to Tiris and Saharawi traditional poets, Mahmud Awah recalls the image of Tiris in the popular tradition as "una tierra en donde no se enferma la gente, y se destaca la longevidad de sus habitantes" ("a land where there is no sickness and where the longevity of the inhabitants stands out"; *Tiris* 60). Tiris, in this memoir and elsewhere in Saharawi writing, is used as a metonymic stand-in for Western Sahara. It represents the memories of the abstract geopolitical entity that features in political and diplomatic wrangling. Conse-quently, it qualifies as a "site of memory" according to the gen-erally accepted understanding of the notion: "any cultural phenomenon, whether material, social or mental, which a so-ciety associates with its past and with national identity" (Erll, *Memory* 25).

Gendered Sites of Memory

Readers will find that they associate Detu with Tiris for rea-sons other than her origins in that region. Her representation in the memoir transforms her into a mnemonic of Tiris and, by extension, of the longed-for land. The parallels between the memory of Tiris and Detu are evident in the stories of nurtur-ing and protection that the author tells about his mother and in the Saharawi values that are embodied in her representa-tion. Mahmud Awah's account of Detu's teaching all her children to read and write and securing his safety by sending him into exile, his allusions to her pain at being separated from him, and the many references to her resourcefulness, her gen-erosity, and her intelligence all resonate with the ideal notion of Saharawi women. Indeed, Mahmud Awah's recollection of how his mother single-handedly took care of the family during the year when his father was held up in El-Aaiún, well before the war, parallels the accounts of how Saharawi women set up and ran the refugee camps while the men were fighting at the front against the Moroccan and Mauritanian occupation. The symbolic link between Detu and Tiris is not difficult to imagine, since Tiris and the Saharawi nation are generally feminized in the memoir and in other Saharawi creative expression (Allan, "Nationalism" 84; Odartey-Wellington 7). In fact, mother and land intersect in the ultimate image of motherhood when Mahmud Awah recalls how Detu had reminded him that he had been raised on the milk of Tirisian camels. In effect, Detu, the central remembering subject in the memoir, like Tiris, is also a site of memory and, as such, an icon that points the way home. Sites are not exclusively spatial in this context; they can also be "events, people and cultural artifacts . . . seen in collective memory as depositaries (symbols) of not one particular value, but of matters important to the community in general, as a 'site' where one finds and can continue finding diverse values" (Szpociński 249).

Mahmud Awah's representation of Detu as a site of memory makes her a significant reference for discussions of the role of gender in Saharawi cultural and collective memory. Indeed, her portrayal in the memoir invites reflection on the feminization of Saharawi national identity, the representations of gender in Saharawi creative expression, and the perspective of Saharawi women on the notion of Saharawi national identity. For example, the prominence given to Detu and other women in the memoir underscores their importance in Saharawi society and refutes colonial and neocolonial representations of Saharawi women, such as those critiqued by Konstantina Isidoros in "Unveiling the Colonial Gaze:

Sahrāwī Women in Nascent Nation-State Formation in the Western Sahara." Paradoxically, Detu's association with Tiris also brings to mind postcolonial feminist criticism of the feminization of territory in gendered nation-building narratives. Critics have drawn attention to the ways in which the woman-nation trope could reproduce sociopolitical norms that narrowly link women to a set of "pre-colonial" cultural values (Stratton 112), generalize rather than individualize women (Boehmer 29), or exclude women whose images do not easily map onto an idealized notion of the nation in question (Odartey-Wellington 13–14). However, the intimate portrayal of Detu, her role as protector and source of vital knowledge, and her own poetic evocations of the territory from which she was exiled all contribute a nuanced perspective to the debate on the symbolic fusion of women and national identity. Furthermore, given the prolonged duration of Saharawis' displacement and the ongoing transformations in Saharawi society and its venues of identity construction, *My Mother, My Teacher* inspires a comparison with the emerging reconfigurations of home and belonging—particularly by transnational Saharawi women—that are identified in Silvia Almenara-Niebla and Carmen Ascanio-Sánchez's "Connected Sahrawi Refugee Diaspora in Spain: Gender, Social Media and Digital Transnational Gossip" and in Allan's "Privilege, Marginalization, and Solidarity: Women's Voices Online in Western Sahara's Struggle for Independence."

Territorial displacement, such as the one in which Saharawis find themselves, endangers cultural heritage. However, *My Mother, My Teacher* illustrates that for Saharawis, the predominantly oral nature of their heritage makes it portable over time and distance. Mahmud Awah gathers within the pages of his memoir a sampling of Saharawi social and cultural practices as well as the media and the venues associated with those practices. He also demonstrates how the re-creation of such practices in exile evokes a sense of continuity and identity with others. The memoir gives literary form to the intangible cultural heritage[9] of Saharawis and further mitigates the threat of loss in their current circumstances. The book both enacts and records the enactments of the transgenerational transmission of traditions, values, creative expression, and local knowledges. Furthermore, it casts a spotlight on a significant aspect of Saharawi imaginations of national identity: gender. All the foregoing signal the ways in which *My Mother, My Teacher* contributes to pointing exiled people in the direction of their home through the eternal art of remembering.

Notes

1. The title of the original Spanish-language publication is *La maestra que me enseñó en una tabla de madera* (*The Woman Who Taught Me on a Wooden Slate*).

2. All translations are mine unless otherwise indicated.

3. See, for example, the special issue of *Ariadna-RC* published in 2004, which is devoted to the culture of Western Sahara (*Memoria*).

4. An archive of short films by graduates of the film school is featured on the website of the Spanish artists' collective Left Hand Rotation ("Escuela").

5. *Polisario* is an acronym for Popular Front for the Liberation of Saguia el-Hamra and Río de Oro (Frente Popular de Liberación de Saguia el-Hamra y Río de Oro). The Polisario, also known as the Polisario Front, was formed in 1973 with the objective of liberating Saharawis from Spanish colonial rule. Mauritania subsequently signed a peace agreement with the Polisario and retreated from Western Sahara in 1979.

6. For more information on Mahmud Awah's personal experience of the exodus from Western Sahara, see the intimate portrait of the writer by his friend and fellow poet Mohamed Salem Abdelfatah in the latter's epilogue to Mahmud Awah's *Versos refugiados*, "Para unos versos refugiados" ("To a Few Refugee Poems").

7. According to a March 2018 report published by the United Nations High Commissioner for Refugees, *Sahrawi Refugees in Tindouf, Algeria: Total In-Camp Population*, that figure is conservative and is to be used solely for planning purposes (5).

8. For more information on the genre, see Voisset.

9. According to UNESCO, intangible cultural heritage includes "traditions or living expressions inherited from our ancestors and passed on to our descendants, such as oral traditions, performing arts, social practices, rituals, festive events, knowledge and practices concerning nature and the universe or the knowledge and skills to produce traditional crafts" ("What").

Works Cited

Allan, Joanna. "Decolonizing Renewable Energy: Aeolian Aesthetics in the Poetry of Fatma Galia Mohammed Salem and Limam Boisha." *Bulletin of Hispanic Studies*, vol. 97, no. 4, 2020, pp. 421–37.

———. "Nationalism, Resistance, and Patriarchy: The Poetry of Saharawi Women." *Hispanic Research Journal*, vol. 12, no. 1, 2011, pp. 78–89.

———. "Privilege, Marginalization, and Solidarity: Women's Voices Online in Western Sahara's Struggle for Independence." *Feminist Media Studies*, vol. 14, no. 4, 2014, pp. 704–08.

Almenara-Niebla, Silvia, and Carmen Ascanio-Sánchez. "Connected Sahrawi Refugee Diaspora in Spain: Gender, Social Media and Digital Transnational Gossip." *European Journal of Cultural Studies*, vol. 23, no. 5, 2020, pp. 768–83.

Anderson, Benedict. *Imagined Communities: Reflections on the Origin and Spread of Nationalism*. Revised ed., Verso, 2006.

Assmann, Jan. "Communicative and Cultural Memory." *A Companion to Cultural Memory Studies*, edited by Astrid Erll and Ansgar Nünning, De Gruyter, 2010, pp. 109–18.

Belgha, la memoria viva. Directed by Man Chagaf, 2008.

Bengochea Tirado, Enrique, and Francesco Correale. "Modernising Violence and Social Change in the Spanish Sahara, 1957–1975." *Itinerario*, vol. 44, no. 1, 2020, pp. 33–54.

Boehmer, Elleke. *Stories of Women: Gender and Narrative in the Postcolonial Nation*. Manchester UP, 2005.

Boisha, Limam. *Ritos de jaima*. Ediciones Bubisher, 2012.

———. *Los versos de madera*. Puentepalo, 2004.

Docherty, Thomas. "Memento Mori." *Irimia et al.*, pp. 50–62.

Ellison, Mahan. "'La Amada Tiris, Tierra de Nuestros Abuelos': The Affective Space of the Sahara in Hispano-Saharawi Literature." *CELAAN: Revue du Centre d'Etudes de Littératures et des Arts d'Afrique du Nord*, vol. 15, nos. 2–3, 2018, pp. 73–102.

Erll, Astri. "Locating Family in Cultural Memory Studies." *Journal of Comparative Family Studies*, vol. 42, no. 3, 2011, pp. 303–18.

———. *Memory in Culture*. Translated by Sara B. Young, Palgrave Macmillan, 2011.

Errazzouki, Samia, and Allison L. McManus, editors. *Beyond Dominant Narratives on the Western Sahara*. Special issue of *JADMAG*. Vol. 1, no. 2, 2013, www.jadmag.org/western-sahara.html.

"Escuela de cine del Sáhara." *Left Hand Rotation*, www.lefthandrotation .com/escuelacinesahara/index.htm. Accessed 8 June 2023.

Faszer-McMahon, Debra. "Images of the Global Hispanophone: Transnational Iconography in Saharaui Literature." *Symposium*, vol. 72, no. 1, 2018, pp. 13–26.

Fernández-Molina, Irene, and Raquel Ojeda-García. "Western Sahara as a Hybrid of a Parastate and a State-in-Exile: (Extra)Territoriality and the Small Print of Sovereignty in a Context of Frozen Conflict." *Nationalities Papers*, vol. 48, no. 1, 2020, pp. 83–99.

Irimia, Mihaela, et al., editors. *Literature and Cultural Memory*. Brill, 2017.

Isidoros, Konstantina. "Unveiling the Colonial Gaze: Sahrāwī Women in Nascent Nation-State Formation in the Western Sahara." *Interventions*, vol. 19, no. 4, 2017, pp. 487–506.

Lacave, Maribel. "Lo que se piensa, se sueña." Mahmud Awah, *Versos refugiados*, pp. 20–24.

Legna: Habla el verso saharaui. Directed by Bahia Mahmud Awah et al., Antropología en Acción ONGD, 2014.

Leyuad: Un viaje al pozo de los versos. Directed by Brahim Chagaf et al., Arbatásh / Ministerio de Cultura R.A.S.D., 2015.

López Martín, Alberto. "Cultural Resistance and Textual Emotionality in the Sahrawi Poetic Anthology *VerSahara*." *Studies in Twentieth- and Twenty-First-Century Literature*, vol. 45, no. 1, 2020, pp. 1–20.

Mahmud Awah, Bahia. "Oral Literature and Transmission in the Sahara." *Quaderns de la Mediterrània*, vol. 13, 2010, pp. 59–64.

———. *El sueño de volver.* CantArabia Editorial, 2012.

———. *Tiris: Rutas literarias.* Última Línea, 2016.

———. *Versos refugiados.* 2nd ed., Bubok Publishing, 2015.

Mahmud Awah, Bahia, and Conchi Moya, editors. *Don Quijote, el azri de la badia saharaui.* Universidad de Alcalá, 2008.

La memoria en la cultura saharaui. Special issue of *Ariadna-RC.* No. 25, 2004, www.ariadna-rc.com/numero25/sahara/sahara.htm.

Moseley, C. W. R. D. "Ancestral Voices." Irimia et al., pp. 63–71.

Odartey-Wellington, Dorothy. "Walls, Borders, and Fences in Hispano-Saharawi Creative Expression." *Research in African Literatures*, vol. 48, no. 3, 2017, pp. 1–17.

Ojeda-García, Raquel, et al., editors. *Global, Regional and Local Dimensions of Western Sahara's Protracted Decolonization: When a Conflict Gets Old.* Palgrave Macmillan, 2017.

Pazzanita, Anthony G., and Tony Hodges. *Historical Dictionary of Western Sahara.* 2nd ed., Scarecrow Press, 1994.

Powell, Katrina M. "Rhetorics of Displacement: Constructing Identities in Forced Relocations." *College English*, vol. 74, no. 4, 2012, pp. 299–324.

Russell, Lynette. "Remembering Places Never Visited: Connections and Context in Imagined and Imaginary Landscapes." *International Journal of Historical Archaeology*, vol. 16, no. 2, 2012, pp. 401–17.

Sahrawi Refugees in Tindouf, Algeria: Total In-Camp Population. United Nations High Commissioner for Refugees, Mar. 2018. *Universidade de Santiago de Compostela*, www.usc.gal/export9/sites/webinsti tucional/gl/institutos/ceso/descargas/UNHCR_Tindouf-Total-In -Camp-Population_March-2018.pdf.

Salem Abdelfatah, Mohamed. *La joven del pozo.* Bubok Publishing, 2009, www.bubok.es/libros/8059/La-joven-del-pozo.

———. "Para unos versos refugiados." Mahmud Awah, *Versos refugiados*, pp. 125–31.

———, editor. *Las voces del viento: Poesía saharaui contemporánea.* Ministerio de Asuntos Exteriores, 2014.

Salem Iselmu, Ali. *Un beduino en el Caribe.* Diputación Provincial de Zaragoza, 2014.

Shelley, Toby. *Endgame in the Western Sahara: What Future for Africa's Last Colony?* Zed Books, 2004.

Stratton, Florence. "'Periodic Embodiments': A Ubiquitous Trope in African Men's Writing." *Research in African Literatures*, vol. 21, no. 1, 1990, pp. 111–26.

Szpociński, Andrzej. "Sites of Memory." *Memory and Place*, special issue of *Teksty*, edited by Justyna Tabaszewska, vol. 1, 2016, pp. 245–54, tekstydrugie.pl/wp-content/uploads/2018/03/Teksty_Drugie_en_2016_-1.pdf.

"III aniversario del Congreso Constituyente de la Generación de la Amistad." *Generación de la Amistad saharaui*, 9 July 2008, generacion delaamistad.blogspot.com/2008/07/aniversario-del-congreso -constituyente.html.

Voisset, Georges M. "The Tebra' of Moorish Women from Mauritania: The Limits (or Essence) of the Poetic Act." *Research in African Literatures*, vol. 24, no. 2, 1993, pp. 79–88.

"What Is Intangible Cultural Heritage?" *UNESCO*, 1992–2023, ich.unesco .org/en/what-is-intangible-heritage-00003.

Zunes, Stephen, and Jacob Mundy. *Western Sahara: War, Nationalism, and Conflict Irresolution.* Syracuse UP, 2010.

ADDITIONAL RESOURCES

Additional Works by Bahia Mahmud Awah

Mahmud Awah, Bahia. *La entidad saharaui precolonial en el ideario de la República Saharaui*. Bubok Publishing, 2017, www.bubok.es/libros/253025/La-entidad-politica -Precolonial-Saharaui.

———, editor. *Literatura del Sahara Occidental: Esbozo histórico*. Bubok Publishing, 2009, www.bubok.es/libros/3818/ Literatura-del-Sahara-Occidental-Breve-estudio.

Mahmud Awah, Bahia, and Conchi Moya. *Cuentos saharauis de mi abuelo*. Bubok Publishing, 2015.

———. *El porvenir del español en el Sahara Occidental: La diversidad lingüística, aspectos antropológicos, sociales y literarios*. Bubok Publishing, 2010, www.bubok.es/libros/ 7470/El-porvenir-del-espanol-en-el-Sahara-Occidental.

Selected Anthologies That Include Works by Bahia Mahmud Awah

La fuente de Saguia: Relatos de la Generación de la Amistad Saharaui. Diputación de Zaragoza / Um Draiga, 2009.

Generación de la Amistad. *Aaiún gritando lo que se siente: Poesía saharaui contemporánea*. Universidad Autónoma de Madrid / Revista Exilios, 2006.

Gewinner, Mick, editor and translator. *Generación de la amistad: Anthologie de poésie sahraouie contemporaine*. L'atelier du Tilde, 2016.

Gimeno Martín, Juan Carlos, et al., editors. *Poetas y poesía del Sahara Occidental: Antología de la poesía nacional saharaui.* Última Línea, 2020.

Miorin, Emanuela, et al., editors. *Le parole non hanno radici: Antología di letteratura saharawi.* Palermo, 2019.

San Martín, Pablo, and Ben Bollig, editors. *Treinta y uno / Thirty One: An Anthology of Saharaui Resistance Poetry.* Sandblast, 2007.

Um Draiga: Poesía saharaui contemporánea. Diputación de Zaragoza / Um Draiga, 2007.

Recommended Reading

Allan, Joanna. "Imagining Saharawi Women: The Question of Gender in Polisario Discourse." *The Journal of North African Studies*, vol. 15, no. 2, 2010, pp. 189–202.

———. *Silenced Resistance: Women, Dictatorships, and Genderwashing in Western Sahara and Equatorial Guinea.* U of Wisconsin P, 2019.

Almenara-Niebla, Silvia. "Making Digital 'Home-Camps': Mediating Emotions among the Sahrawi Refugee Diaspora." *International Journal of Cultural Studies*, vol. 23, no. 5, 2020, pp. 728–44.

Álvarez Gila, Oscar, et al. "Western Sahara: Migration, Exile and Environment." *International Migration*, vol. 49, supp. s1, 2011, pp. e146–e163.

Baers, Michael. "Concerning Intent, Interpretation, Memory and Ambiguity in the Work of an Informal Collective Working on the Western Sahara Conflict." *Memory Studies*, vol. 12, no. 3, 2019, pp. 294–306.

Berkson, Sam, and Mohamed Sulaiman. *Settled Wanderers.* Influx Press, 2015.

Campos-Serrano, Alicia, and José Antonio Rodríguez-Esteban. "Imagined Territories and Histories in Conflict during the

Struggles for Western Sahara, 1956–1979." *Journal of Historical Geography*, vol. 55, 2017, pp. 44–59.

Campoy-Cubillo, Adolfo. "Walking through the Sahrawi Refugee Camps with Judith Butler." Robbins and Campoy-Cubillo, *Sahara*, pp. 166–78, https://doi.org/10.5070/T453029641.

Chatty, Dawn, et al. "Identity with/out Territory: Sahrawi Refugee Youth in Transnational Space." *Deterritorialized Youth: Sahrawi and Afghan Refugees at the Margins of the Middle East*, edited by Chatty, Berghahn Books, 2010, pp. 37–84.

Deubel, Tara Flynn. "Mediascapes of Human Rights: Emergent Forms of Digital Activism for the Western Sahara." Robbins and Campoy-Cubillo, *Sahara*, pp. 5–19, https://doi.org/10.5070/T453029633.

———. "Poetics of Diaspora: Sahrawi Poets and Postcolonial Transformations of a Trans-Saharan Genre in Northwest Africa." *The Journal of North African Studies*, vol. 17, no. 2, 2012, pp. 295–314.

Drury, Mark. "Disidentification with Nationalist Conflict: Loyalty and Mobility in Moroccan-Occupied Western Sahara." *Comparative Studies of South Asia, Africa, and the Middle East*, vol. 40, no. 1, 2020, pp. 133–49.

Farah, Randa. "Sovereignty on Borrowed Territory: Sahrawi Identity in Algeria." *Georgetown Journal of International Affairs*, vol. 11, no. 2, 2010, pp. 59–66.

Faszer-McMahon, Debra. "African Poetics in Spain: *Um Draiga* and the Voices of Contemporary Saharawi Poetry." *African Immigrants in Contemporary Spanish Texts: Crossing the Strait*, edited by Faszer-McMahon and Victoria L. Ketz, Ashgate, 2015, pp. 223–40.

———. "Poetics and Politics: Digital Interventions in Sahrawi Cultural Production." Robbins and Campoy-Cubillo, *Sahara*, pp. 20–39, https://doi.org/10.5070/T453029634.

Fiddian-Qasmiyeh, Elena. *The Ideal Refugees: Gender, Islam and the Sahrawi Politics of Survival.* Syracuse UP, 2014.

———. "The Inter-generational Politics of 'Travelling Memories': Sahrawi Refugee Youth Remembering Home-Land and Home-Camp." *Journal of Intercultural Studies,* vol. 34, no. 6, 2013, pp. 631–49.

Finden, Alice. "Active Women and Ideal Refugees: Dissecting Gender, Identity and Discourse in the Sahrawi Refugee Camps." *Feminist Review,* vol. 120, no. 1, 2018, pp. 37–53.

Herz, Manuel, editor. *From Camp to City: Refugee Camps of the Western Sahara.* Lars Müller Publishers, 2013.

Isidoros, Konstantina. *Nomads and Nation-Building in the Western Sahara: Gender, Politics and the Sahrawi.* Bloomsbury Publishing, 2018.

———. "The View from Tindouf: Western Saharan Women and the Calculation of Autochthony." *Global, Regional and Local Dimensions of Western Sahara's Protracted Decolonization: When a Conflict Gets Old,* edited by Raquel Ojeda-García et al., Palgrave Macmillan, 2017, pp. 295–311.

Karaoud, Amira. "War, Culture, and Agency among Sahrawi Women Refugees: A Photo-Essay." *Gender and the Media: Women's Places,* edited by Marcia Texler Segal and Vasilikie Demos, Emerald Publishing, 2018, pp. 15–27.

Lippert, Anne. "Sahrawi Women in the Liberation Struggle of the Sahrawi People." *Signs: Journal of Women in Culture and Society,* vol. 17, no. 3, 1992, pp. 636–51.

López Belloso, María, and Irantzu Mendia Azkue. "Local Human Development in Contexts of Permanent Crisis: Women's Experiences in the Western Sahara." *Jamba,* vol. 2, no. 3, 2009, pp. 159–76.

Martin-Márquez, Susan. "Brothers and Others: Fraternal Rhetoric and the Negotiation of Spanish and Saharawi Identity." *Journal of Spanish Cultural Studies,* vol. 7, no. 3, 2006, pp. 241–58.

Murphy, Jennifer M., and Sidi M. Omar. "Aesthetics of
Resistance in Western Sahara." *Peace Review*, vol. 25, no. 3,
2013, pp. 349–58.

Robbins, Jill. "Celebrity, Diplomacy, Documentary: Javier
Bardem and *Sons of the Clouds: The Last Colony*." Robbins
and Campoy-Cubillo, *Sahara*, pp. 100–17, https://doi.org/10
.5070/T453029638.

Robbins, Jill, and Adolfo Campoy-Cubillo. "Considering the
Western Sahara: Multi-disciplinary Approaches to Post-
colonialism." Robbins and Campoy-Cubillo, *Sahara*,
pp. 1–4, https://doi.org/10.5070/T453029632.

———, editors. *Sahara*. Special issue of *Transmodernity:
Journal of Peripheral Cultural Production of the Luso-Hispanic
World*. Vol. 5, no. 3, 2015.

Rossetti, Sonia. "Saharawi Women and Their Voices as
Political Representatives Abroad." *The Journal of North
African Studies*, vol. 17, no. 2, 2012, pp. 337–53.

Ruano Posada, Violeta, and Vivian Solana Moreno. "The
Strategy of Style: Music, Struggle, and the Aesthetics of
Sahrawi Nationalism in Exile." Robbins and Campoy-
Cubillo, *Sahara*, pp. 40–61, https://doi.org/10.5070/
T453029635.

San Martín, Pablo. "'¡Estos Locos Cubarauis!': The
Hispanisation of Saharawi Society (. . . after Spain)." *Journal
of Transatlantic Studies*, vol. 7, no. 3, 2009, pp. 249–63.

———. *Western Sahara: The Refugee Nation*. U of Wales P, 2010.

Sayahi, Lofti. "España ante el Mundo: Spain's Colonial
Language Policies in North Africa." Robbins and Campoy-
Cubillo, *Sahara*, pp. 62–75, https://doi.org/10.5070/
T453029636.

Solana, Vivian. "Between Publics and Privates: The
Regeneration of Sahrawi Female Militancy." *Comparative
Studies of South Asia, Africa, and the Middle East*, vol. 40,
no. 1, 2020, pp. 150–65.

———. "Hospitality's Prowess: Performing Sahrāwī
Sovereignty in Refugee Camps." *Political and Legal
Anthropology Review*, vol. 42, no. 2, 2019, pp. 362–79.

Suárez Collado, Ángela, and Raquel Ojeda García. "The
Effects of the Moroccan Advanced Regionalization Process
in Western Sahara." Robbins and Campoy-Cubillo, *Sahara*,
pp. 76–98, https://doi.org/10.5070/T453029637.

Recommended Viewing

La Badil. Directed by Dominic Brown, Dancing Turtle Films,
2012.

Diáspora en el Sahara. Directed by Ignacio Rosselló and Néstor
Suleiman, Instituto Nacional de Cine y Artes
Audiovisuales, 2018.

Hamada. Directed by Eloy Domínguez Serén, Momento
Film, 2018.

Hijos de las nubes: La última colonia. Directed by Álvaro
Longoria, Morena Films, 2012.

Life Is Waiting: Referendum and Resistance in Western Sahara.
Directed by Iara Lee, Caipirinha Productions, 2015.

The Oasis of Memory: Fragments of Sahrawi Culture. Directed by
Elisa Mereghetti and Marco Mensa, Ethnos Films, 2003.

Oulaya's Wedding. Directed by Hisham Mayet et al., Sublime
Frequencies, 2017.

El rumor de la arena. Directed by Daniel Iriarte and Jesús
Prieto, Atila Films, 2008.

The Runner. Directed by Saeed Taji Farouky, Creative Visions /
Underground Films, 2013.

Skeikima. Directed by Raquel Larrosa and María Alonso, 2017.

Song of Umm Dalaila: The Story of the Saharawis. Directed by
Danielle Smith, Dakkuma Productions, 1993.

Wilaya. Directed by Pedro Pérez Rosado, Wanda Visión, 2011.

Note on the Translation

Translating a work of literature into a language that is widely spoken means bringing a culture to the table in global conversations. The barrier faced by Saharawi authors who write in Spanish in bringing their works to a global readership is not simply a linguistic one. After all, Spanish is spoken by 572 million people worldwide, according to Instituto Cervantes ("Notas"). Saharawi writers are isolated because of geopolitical factors stemming from a failed decolonization process and its aftermath: occupation and exile. The Moroccan occupation of Western Sahara, which has lasted over forty years and which has sent several Saharawis into exile in Algeria, Spain, and elsewhere, has kept the former Spanish colony's writers on the margins of the institutions that facilitate the dissemination of culture. Thus, although the voices of these writers spring forth from significant global events, their stories tend to be invisible in debates on issues generated by said events, such as displacement, migration, exile, identity, and memory making, to name a few. This translation, therefore, aims to bring Bahia Mahmud Awah's work, which resonates with the abovementioned themes, to a wider readership.

The current translation is based on Mahmud Awah's revised version of the original 2011 work, *La maestra que me enseñó en una tabla de madera* (*The Woman Who Taught Me on a Wooden Slate*). The revised version includes an epilogue written by the author, in which he provides new information from research that he carried out subsequent to the 2011 publication. In translating this work, one is faced not only with the translation of the text from Spanish into English but also with the more significant challenge of translating Saharawi culture and its manifestations in the orality of Mahmud Awah's memoir. The text's orality is reflected in the author's use of Hassaniya transliterations to render concepts and expressions that are peculiar to the Saharawi culture and worldview. It is also present in the Saharawi oral tradition—family stories, oral poems, and sayings—at the core of social and familial interactions in the work. With this in mind, I was guided by the principle of making Saharawi culture accessible to an anglophone readership without losing its emotion, spirit, and rhythm. I have tried to maintain a fine balance between what translation scholars call foreignization—"the preservation of cultural difference" (Ettobi 227)—and domestication.

To this end, I have retained the transliterations of Hassaniya wherever they appear in the original text. To do otherwise would be to erase a wider world of experiences made available through the source culture. For example, to translate the portable nomadic Saharawi dwelling, *jaima,* as "tent" in any language would be tantamount to referring to the homes of urban dwellers as mere "buildings." Similarly, a word such as *amshakab* cannot be rendered simply as "saddle," since it refers to a particular kind of saddle, one that is specifically for women and used as storage for food and utensils. As the author did in the original, I provide a glossary at the end of the translation. (Terms that appear in the glossary are indicated with italics.) These Hassaniya expressions and the glossary provide an additional layer of insight into Saharawi culture and worldview. Furthermore, to reflect the work's bilingual and transcultural character, I have reproduced the poems in Arabic script that are interspersed in the original work. Each of the poems is followed by a translation that is based on the Spanish translation provided by the author in the original.

My translation of Mahmud Awah's memoir resonates with what Mieke Bal describes as "accented translation," by which she means "translation that bears the traces, the remainder, of what is itself a translation as well as of that translated status of its 'original'" (111). Although Bal's observations were inspired by translation in film, they lend themselves to textual expression as well. My work is a translation of a translation for two reasons. First, on a literal level it involves the rendering in English of thoughts and creative expression that the author had previously translated into Spanish from Hassaniya. Second, the source text is itself the result of a translation of orality into textuality. The traces of Saharawi "accent" and orality in my translation protect distinct elements of Saharawi culture from being effaced through domestication.

Mahmud Awah's notes to the text, which I have translated here into English, are indicated with roman numerals. My own notes are indicated with arabic numerals.

Note

A version of my translation of the section titled "The Story of How My Grandfather Omar Almost Starved to Death" was published in *The Savannah Review*, no. 4, 2014, pp. 75–82, and in the online magazine *Culture Trip*.

Works Cited

Bal, Mieke. "Translating Translation." *Journal of Visual Culture*, vol. 6, no. 1, 2007, pp. 109–24.

Ettobi, Mustapha. "Translating Orality in the Postcolonial Arabic Novel: A Study of Two Cases of Translation into English and French." *Translation Studies*, vol. 8, no. 2, 2015, pp. 226–40.

"Notas de prensa." *Instituto Cervantes*, 1991–2023, www.cervantes.es/ sobre_instituto_cervantes/prensa/2017/noticias/Presentaci%C3 %B3n-Anuario-2017.htm.

My Mother, My Teacher:
A Memoir from Western Sahara

To Mama—forever in my heart—and to all mothers

Children are the anchors that connect mothers to life.
—Sophocles

Contents

I.

My Mother Was My Teacher

Mother, the most beautiful word pronounced by
humankind. The most beautiful word on the lips
of a man is the word mother, and the sweetest call is:
oh, mother.

—Khalil Gibran

My mother was born in 1942 in the valley of Bu Lariah, a famous mountain located on the southern plateau of Tiris, known as white Tiris. She was the daughter of Omar and Nisha, who had eight children, and she came after Alati, the firstborn and the son of Omar's first wife.

At the age of fifteen, she met my father in the valley of Aboilay, near the Leyuad hills, where her family—*Ahel Omar Uld Ali Uld Embarek Fal*—had set up their *frig*. A year later, she married my father. She told me this story in August 2006.

Her name was Jadiyetu, but I normally did not say her full name. I used to call her by what her name sounded like to me when I was little, "Detu," and I also called her "Mama" in Spanish, because she knew a lot of words in our second language. And so, to this very day, she is simply "Mama" or "Detu" to me.

5

On October 20, 2006, my mother, the teacher who taught me my first letters of the alphabet on the brown wooden board we call a *louh*, passed away. There are eight of us siblings, and she taught us all how to read and write—except the youngest of my sisters, Salca, who was born in 1981 in the Saharawi refugee camps.

I learned a lot of stories from my mother by listening to her at the pleasant gatherings that she held on countless occasions with family and friends. She was an inexhaustible source of anecdotes, tales, and stories; she was essentially an encyclopedia of Hassaniya[1] and Arabic literature.

She told us that in 1958, when Spain and France were vying to control the territory and draw up the colonial boundaries, they would bomb people's *frig* and their livestock. They would also drop hundreds of Arabic pamphlets from their planes, saying that all Saharawis were to move further inland to avoid the clashes that were going on along the French-Spanish colonial borders with the armed bands that had infiltrated the area through the northern border. She was the only person in her *frig* who really knew how to read. At night, her brothers would come down from the mountains, where they would all be hiding in fear of the planes, to collect the pamphlets. She would then read them out to inform the other no-

---

1. The Saharawi language. It derives from Classical Arabic.

6

mads, who were also camping there, of the warnings that had been issued by the colonial powers.

One day, at dawn, the Spanish airplanes dropped some boxes that opened up and spilled out some pamphlets with a message written in Arabic and Spanish. No one among those Bedouins could read, except the young girl who years later would become my mother. Her older brother and the herders collected the leaflets during the night and took them to her so that she could read the announcement to them: "Attention all Saharawis. Move deeper into the territory and stay away from the borders."

She would have no knowledge of my whereabouts for ten years—from the winter of 1975, when I was separated from her by the war at the age of fifteen, until I saw her again in the summer of 1985. But in my interactions with Detu, I never felt like the grown man that I had become. She became Mother Courage when she took that decision in the heat of the war: "Get out of here and go with the Polisario. They will take care of you. Those people who are attacking us will kill you." She felt that her brother, Mohamed Fadel "Boiba," who had deserted from the Spanish army in 1974 and joined the ranks of the Polisario, would protect me in my flight. My flight into exile, and her not having the slightest idea of what had become of me, caused her a great deal of suffering while she was living under the occupation.

To her, I was forever that bumbling, funny, innocent child who would always make her laugh when she least expected to. She used to say that I was fearless as a child and that my father's friends would often come over to our house to prank me and laugh at my childish antics. As a grown man, I didn't change that relationship. I knew that it made her feel very good because it took her back and kept her close to the old days when I was a child and she a young woman. Everything that I know about Hassaniya and Arabic literature is from the many lessons that she gave me in our *jaima* or in our house in Auserd. She loved Tiris very much and knew the region like the back of her hand. She had memorized the names of obscure parts of the land, and she knew the history of all the poets who eulogized Tiris, such as Chej Mohamed El Mami, Emhamed Uld Tolba, Shmeidra Uld Habibulah, Chej Eluali, or Badi Uld Mohamed Salem, whom she knew personally. She also admired Sedum Uld Endarti, the Mauritanian poet and traditional singer-songwriter who identified with Saharawi society all his life. She used to call him "Sedum the Great," because there was another singer from the same family who was also called Sedum.

I remember that in 1973, my school in Auserd invited us to spend the summer in Castellón de la Plana,[2] but she

---

2. A city in the Autonomous Community of Valencia, Spain.

wouldn't let me go because she was worried that something might happen to me. My teacher Francisco, or "Paco," as we used to call him, went to my house to talk to her, and he reassured her that I would be all right and that nothing would happen to me. Finally, my mother consented, and I remember her saying to him over and over again, "Francisco, if they steal him from me or if he goes missing, I will hold you responsible." And to think that when I returned from that unforgettable vacation, I didn't tell her that I had gotten lost one night and that it was the Guardia Civil[3] that picked me up and took me back to the hostel where we were staying.

I wanted to remain forever young for her. I felt that otherwise, I could lose that childlike friendship that had kept us close since my infancy. I used to tell her all my secrets, and I would get her talking about any topic that interested me. My mother was not one for frivolous gossip, which we call *asuaka* in Hassaniya. When a conversation was not to her liking, she would discreetly walk away. She did not like complainers, people who made too much noise and got in the way of good neighborliness. She had a saying in that regard, which goes: "Get to know your neighbor well before setting up camp."

---

3. The Guardia Civil (Civil Guard) is a Spanish national law enforcement and security force.

Her memory and skill in the oral tradition were amazing. She had memorized, in the original Arabic, almost the entire story of the poet-prince Kais Ibnu Al Mulauah, an anonymous work whose Western equivalent is the tragedy of Romeo and Juliet, by William Shakespeare, and which is also known in another Arabic version as "Madjnun Leyla."[4] Legend has it that around the eighth century in the Arabian Peninsula, a Bedouin poet by the name of Kais became famous for his poems. Kais fell in love with his pretty young cousin Leyla, but when the family did not accept their relationship, Kais lost his mind and wandered through the countryside singing to Leyla the most beautiful poems ever known to Arabic lyric poetry. My mother even knew the inspiration for each poem that Kais had dedicated to his beloved Leyla. I recall that, in early 1975, Mama enrolled me in private Classical Arabic poetry classes that were taught nightly by a Mauritanian teacher. She maintained that for a man to be able to engage in conversation and make a good impression, he had to memorize hundreds of poems and know how to recite and draw on them to discuss any topic that was relevant to the conversation.

She was also accomplished at reciting notable poems by great Hassaniya poets such as Badi Mohamed Salem

---

4. "Layla and Majnun."

and his brother, Chej Mohamed El Mami; Salama Uld Ye-
dahlu; and other renowned poets from the Chej Malainin
family, who all sang about Tiris in their time. And her
talents in that area were not limited to Saharawi poets,
because when she heard a Hassaniya poem from neighboring Mauritania she would name the composer right
away, without missing a beat. At her social gatherings,
she spoke as if she were reciting poetry, with a voice that
was measured, calm, gentle, and very firm.

In her final years living as a refugee, my mother would
on many occasions turn to this poem by Badi, which she
would recite, pleading with God to allow her to see the
hills of Tiris again—those hills that are extolled by the poet
but that today are desolate and inhabited by Moroccan soldiers who are alien to our land.

مايدوم اعلي حال أمال	مارت إن الدهر العضار
أجوير و دار اغزومال	ذيك دار اطرطاك ؤدار
و لاتل في العب انوال	خاليات الا ماهي نار
يالعكل افلعليب افريك	و لا التليت اتشوف امطاليك
الناس ؤ لا كثرت مال	و لا اتليت اتشوف زين

It is evident
that time is treacherous,
it is not permanent,
because over there,

11

in Tartag and in Ayueir,
we once had our campsites,
and over there, in Agzumal,
other ones now deserted,
without campfires or traces of life among the dunes,
without migrating herds, or you, oh my love,
walking freely, and leisurely, among the dunes.
And now, we no longer see
the most beautiful woman of *lefrig*,
nor bountiful herds.

Her kindness to vulnerable people always far exceeded her means. I remember that once, back in the sixties, she bankrupted our small family business, a shop that sold clothing, women's cosmetics, and honey that my father imported from Mauritania. Detu would sell on credit to people who had no money, and in the end our capital began to dwindle as we lost our profits to the unpaid debts. Even so, people who knew her well used to say that she was my father's eyes and brains for the thirty-one years that she was with him until they separated in 1988 when they were refugees in Algeria.

I have been separated many times, throughout our perilous lives, from my family and from my mother. I once again felt that overwhelming sensation of being orphaned when I traveled to Spain. Fortunately, that feeling abated thanks to the support and help that I received from other families who became mine too. In 1999, when I arrived in Madrid from the Saharawi refugee camps in Algeria to take a course in journalism at Cadena SER,[5] I met a German woman who practically became my second mother, filling the void that I had endured ever since I was separated from my family and especially from Mama. I lived with her and her daughter Irene for a month in a lovely neighborhood in Madrid and, in their company, I felt as if I was with my own family, because they showed me all the love and care that I needed. Christa Michael, her daughter Irene, and their cats—two typical felines called Pío and Galatea, who slept in each other's embrace—were the embodiment of all the affection and the kindness that permeated their home.

By nature, we Saharawis feel very comfortable and welcome depending on what we see in the eyes of our host. If they show affection and happiness, we know right away that we are welcome, and if not, we find a way to slip away. We value a happy face and friendship more than insincere material gifts.

Christa's affection felt like that of a real mother to me that afternoon when I was about to move out to an apartment on calle de la Ballesta, which was situated right

---

5. A Spanish radio network.

behind the Cadena SER headquarters in the Gran Vía building at number 32. That afternoon, I told my second mother that I was moving out to my new place. In response, Christa simply asked me to accompany her to the supermarket to do the groceries, which we often did together. But that afternoon, unbeknownst to me at the time, we were not going to be doing her usual household groceries.

We returned home after the errand, and I had to finish my light packing, just one suitcase, since I planned to leave behind some clothes that I did not need. I figured that if I needed them at some point, I would go back to Mama Christa's to get them.

I picked up my suitcase and was about to say goodbye when Christa came out of the kitchen with all the shopping that we had just done and said to me, "Here, take this with you, you're going to need it."

It had everything, and I told her that I couldn't accept it, but between my noes and her yeses I finally agreed to take it all with me to my new place, and by the way, all those groceries came in handy after a week in my new home.

This gesture reminded me of the many times that my mother was in that role, packing some water and food for me on the days when I was going out to herd the livestock in the desert, or when I was going mountain climbing in the Auserd hills with my friends from school. That unforgettable and humane gesture could only be a sign of love from a person who felt my pain and my suffering, a person who was concerned that I might go hungry or run out of supplies and who knew that she was my only source of support at the time.

I am thankful to Mama Christa, who took me in at that extremely difficult stage of my life when I had neither immigration documents nor employment, although I did have a lot of strength and ambition for a brighter future. I have expressed my gratitude to her many times, but I don't think I will ever be able to thank her enough.

I had arrived at Christa's from the home of Rosa Saranova and Josan Cousilla, also great friends of mine and of the Saharawi cause, with whom I stayed during my first few weeks on Spanish soil. I lived with them in Benidorm, which was my first haven of support. I had met Rosa and her daughter some time before in the Saharawi liberated territories and refugee camps. We became friends there, and I remember with special fondness an excursion that we took together to explore the liberated territories, specifically Tifariti, and the Ajshash region. We shared some nights of real friendship with the Bedouin nomads around the glow of a campfire while watching the camels resting next to their owners. They also helped me a lot. I recall that my very first computer course was in Benidorm, and Rosa and Josan paid for it. I will also always remember the attention that they showered on me during the time when I would go back and forth to their lovely *jaima* on calle Flores.

They told me that Josan was in El-Aaiún during Spain's final years in the Sahara and that he had been exiled to the Sahara during the Franco regime[6] because of his political activism in the Communist Party of Spain. Rosa was one of the first women to become a traffic services officer in El-Aaiún and in all of Spain. Her love for the Saharawi people originates from those times. To me, they too were a real source of support and are a family that loves me very much.

I should also mention that during that trip to the liberated territories, I met Leire Pajín, Secretary of State for Cooperation in the first José Luis Rodríguez Zapatero government.[7] Leire was studying sociology at the University of Alicante when I met her. She, her sister Amaya, and Rosa Saranova sent me a fax when they returned to Spain to inform me that they had formed an Association of Friends of the Saharawi People in Benidorm. They named it "Martyr Juita," which is how I had nicknamed our excursion to

---

6. General Francisco Franco ruled Spain, as a dictator, from the end of the Spanish Civil War (1936–39) until his death in 1975.

7. José Luis Rodríguez Zapatero was prime minister of Spain for two terms, from 2004 to 2011.

the liberated territories, in honor of a Saharawi activist who was murdered in the Moroccan prisons in the 1980s for opposing the occupation of the Sahara.

I remember a very challenging incident that occurred on that trip as we were making our way back to the camps. We decided to travel at night in order to camp halfway there in an area near Bir Lehlu, where there were many acacias, and to sleep out there in the open. The driver of the car in which Leire and Rosa were traveling, however, got lost and went the wrong way. He overtook the other convoy and drove all night with his passengers until he found himself, the following morning, near a Saharawi military station some twenty kilometers from the guest center.

I was the leader of the excursion, and I felt terrible. I feared that something serious had happened to the group. I pictured the car overturned on an embankment along the road and its occupants helpless in the middle of the night. As we were searching for our missing companions, we went back onto the road and climbed up to higher ground to signal by flashing our headlights, checking the possible routes that the group might have taken. Luckily, we went up to a military checkpoint, where we were reassured with news that the white four-wheel drive had driven by hours earlier in the direction of Rabouni. I felt so relieved in that moment!

When I returned from the trip, I told my mother about the excursion and how beautiful the Ajshash region is, with its camels and Bedouins. And in response, she said to me, "I dreamed that something had happened to you and that you were worried, but I didn't make much of it. It was just a dream."

Then I told her what had really happened to us. She used to tell me that oftentimes dreams subsequently turned into real-life events. My sister Nana explained that vision or premonition that Mama had with a Saharawi expression that goes something like this: "There is something about Mama." By that, she meant that our mother could see the future.

Regarding Detu's counsel, my father maintained that whenever family members did not listen to her on certain matters, things almost always turned out badly. My father was aware that there was a great deal of wisdom in Mama's ideas. He recognized the fact that our mother was sensible and also better educated and more knowledgeable than he was, which is why he said he always discussed everything with her and sought her opinion, even if he didn't always listen to her.

The last time I was with Detu was during Holy Week in 2006, and she looked tired and weak to me. It was obvious that the years of exile were taking their toll on her. I had really been looking forward to recording some stories with her for my research project, but she wasn't feeling well. A few weeks later, after I returned to Madrid, I would speak to her regularly on the phone. By then she was feeling much better and exhibiting her usual lucidity and good sense of humor.

We took the opportunity, at the time, to talk almost every week. Detu would recite some poems to me on the phone, and I would ask about other family stories and discuss with her the tales, anecdotes, and names of certain places and characters in Hassaniya literature. My mother conversed very lucidly, explaining even small, less significant details, because, in her opinion, minor events were also important when it came to passing on credible and substantiated stories.

She kept her voice firm and cheerful, and she would have a good laugh over some surprising questions that I asked her for the first time, such as "Mama, where did you meet my father?," to which she responded, "He was brought to us by Agmeini Uld Nayem in Aboilay Leyuad." Agmeini was a close friend of my father's. I really laughed at the way that she began her response: "He was brought to us . . ." It was unusual to ask one's parents such a question in Saharawi culture, but it shows how close I was to her.

In July 2006 I rented a comfortable house for her in Tindouf so that she could spend the summer there away

19

from the extremely high temperatures that the refugees endure, as always with her poor and fragile health in mind. However, a month and a half later, my sisters called to tell me that Mama wanted to return to her *jaima*. I spoke to her to let her know that it was still very hot and that she ought to wait until after the harshest days in August, but she said to me, "I am leaving for the camps where I have my *jaima*. I am already feeling quite well." I tried to persuade her to stay until it got cooler, around October, but I had to respect her decision as I had always done. Detu had a weak heart, because she had suffered from asthma since she was very young and because of her natural constitution, which made her very thin and frail.

I have always felt that my personality embodies hers. She was sociable, affectionate, kind, made friends wherever she went, and was incapable of hating or holding a grudge against anyone. On Friday, October 20, which was the twenty-seventh day of Ramadan, she went to visit her mother, my grandmother Nisha. After having some tea, Detu presented her holiday gifts to Nisha and asked for her blessing. Moments later she passed away from a heart attack. She will always be present in my heart with the same love that she taught me to have for her.

II.

MEMORIES AND MEMENTOS:

OUR OLD FRIENDS

My memories of Mama will continue to beat in my heart forever through the resonance of her ideas, her human qualities, her kindness, and the protection that she gave to those who needed her. I feel strongly that her life did not end with the prayers of farewell that were said in the land of exile, nor with the tears that we shed over our irreversible loss.

She was the *talha* with a luxuriant and verdant crown laden with *anish* and *eljarrub*. And that is how those of us who rested under her welcoming and timely shade will remember her.

With these memories I would like to pay a posthumous tribute to the person that I have loved most in all my life. Since I was a child, my relationship with Mama was not just the natural relationship between a mother and son. There was far more than that maternal bond between us. She was my mother, my teacher, my accomplice, my friend, and my guardian angel at critical times in my life. She rescued me countless times when I was on the brink of dying of thirst during the harsh desert summers; and countless times she kept vigil over my moaning as an ailing child, soothing my pain with the scent of her *melhfa*.

I have felt her absence during these past few years of my exile. I have missed hearing her conversation amid the sounds of our traditional tea ceremony, with her pleasant comments, her critique, and her clear-eyed view of our society—a society shattered by an unjust war that was forced upon it and that has broken up our families, separating friends, siblings, and parents from their children and sending so many into exile, far away from their roots.

Mama lost her father when she had just turned sixteen. Her mother, my grandmother Nisha, was a strong, good, and very intelligent woman who was able to educate all her children and fight for them during other difficult times until they became adults. And all together, they held up high the *Ahel* Omar Ali Embarek Fal name. Two of Detu's siblings remained in the cities occupied by Morocco. Alati Omar, her older brother, died in the occupied city of El-Aaiún without their ever being able to meet again. Her sister Boilili still lives in the occupied city of Bojador. Her other six siblings and her mother, my grandmother Nisha, still live in the Saharawi refugee camps in southern Algeria.

My Grandmother Nisha in the Desert
without Any Water

My grandmother Nisha was a woman who, from a very early age, had been toughened up by the scourges and adversities inflicted by nature on the *badia* and who knew everything about the geography and the flora and fauna of the territory. She was the center around which the whole family revolved, since she had been widowed at a time when she was still young and strong. According to my uncle Moulud, the family had once camped in the region of Eselb, near the town of Bir Enzaran—it must have been around 1971—during a very harsh and hot summer in central Tiris. Nisha's older sons, Alati and Mohamed, got their camels ready to travel very far away to get water, a journey known among the Bedouins as *errualla*. The journey to find water can take a day if the wells are not far away, but sometimes the search becomes difficult and takes much longer than expected. Nisha stayed behind with the rest of the family and her two small grandchildren, my cousin Ehmoidilat and my brother Muhamiyu, who was raised from early childhood by my grandmother.

Several days went by with no sign of the *errualla*; meanwhile, the water that my grandmother had was running out, despite her strict rationing as she tried to buy time until her sons returned with the water. But the summer heat, with its *smayem*-time *irifi*, was overpowering for both the most daring and the most cautious, especially at that point in the season. It left the animals dehydrated and put their owners at risk. The two children would not stop crying for water, and she kept trying to calm them down and keep them from getting dehydrated by giving them little sips of water from one of those tiny glasses that are used for preparing tea. Finally, she decided to tuck them under her *amshakab*, because it was a little more protected from the sun there and a bit more humid.

With the children under her *amshakab*, she waited all day while giving them the little sips of water, which she would later mix with a bit of sour camel milk to alleviate their hunger pangs. She was waiting for nightfall, when the air would cool down and when she might see a *deyar* approaching with a bowl of milk or water. She endured the whole night, fervently hoping that her sons would appear with the water, because if they spent one more day alone, she was certain that her two grandchildren would die.

She called upon God and all the saints to help her before tragedy struck. At the first rays of light the following morning, Nisha sighted the silhouettes of two camel riders speeding toward the *jaima*, but her eyes were so bleary from the thirst that she had endured during the three days of waiting that she couldn't tell for sure if they were her sons. Indeed, it was Alati and Mohamed, returning just in time with the water. This is one of the stories that my uncles most remember, as does my cousin Ehmoidilat, since he experienced it firsthand and remembers it in great detail.

Mariam Mint Mohamed Chej

Mama had two other children whom she raised in the 1970s from when they were only a few months old—Mohamed Yeslem Beisat and El Hafed—in addition to the eight of us. Their mother, Mariam Mohamed Chej Maatala, was her best friend in her youth. She was also the sister of Hanafi Mohamed Chej Maatala, a member of the legendary first generation of young Saharawi university students in the colonial era who founded the Polisario.

I met Hanafi in Castellón de la Plana in the summer of 1973 when I was thirteen years old, but I didn't know that he was related to my mother's friend. I remember that he came to meet us at the Valencia airport that summer. I was on my way back from a vacation that had been organized by the youth movement and sponsored by the General Government of the Sahara, which was a Spanish province at the time. Hanafi was one of the most prominent Saharawi students in the ranks of the Polisario during the early years of the movement. He fell in battle in the 1970s when he was still a very young leader. His sister Mariam, Mohamed Yeslem and El Hafed's mother, was an extraordinarily beautiful woman who inspired this next poem, which her life partner, Beisat Uld Deish Uld Boyda, used to recite to her. Mariam, her brother Hanafi, and her husband, Beisat, are all resting in peace now. I had always thought that Beisat himself had composed the poem until I discovered in my research that it was the work of the Mauritanian poet El Mojtar Uld Haddar. Perhaps to Beisat, a man of letters well versed in Saharawi literature and a Hassaniya poet, that poem sounded personal because it mentioned his wife's name the way he affectionately called her: Mrayuma, the affectionate diminutive of Mariam.

اعلي لبن البل عت طاب   و اعلي امريوما نوما

و الدنيا كاع الل اشراب   لبن البل و امريوما نوما

Accustomed to my camels' milk,
accustomed to Mrayuma's love.
And this life,
is all a sweet beverage,
like camel milk,
when I am with Mrayuma.

My mother used to recite the poem to her friends, with whom she enjoyed pleasant and entertaining conversations amid the sound of the skillful performance of the Saharawi tea ceremony, the main event at the gatherings. I learned the poem when I was thirteen, and it became etched in my memory forever because it reflects how loyal Mama's friendship with her best friend was. That poem will always remind us of the two of them.

According to my aunt El Iza, when Mariam fell ill, she was living in Auserd, away from her husband, Beisat, who was being held prisoner by the Moroccan army in El-Aaiún. This was during the first few months of the occupation of the Sahara, and he was not allowed to go and see her in Auserd, which was then under Mauritanian control. As I have already mentioned, Beisat was a good orator and poet. He pleaded with the occupiers several times to let him go and see his ailing wife. Time was against him, and desperate to see his wife, he sought refuge in this beautiful poem, titled "The Desire of My Soul," which he dedicated to her.

غي عند الحكوما

لخلاك الليل داير

نلك فيهم مريوما

ساعا وربع في الطاير

From the depths of darkness,
my soul demands from that power,
an hour and fifteen minutes by air
to be with my Mrayuma again.

27

Hanafi

Detu used to tell a story about the exceptional handsomeness of the prophet Dauda—David in the Bible—and when I first met Hanafi Uld Mohamed Chej in 1973, the image of the prophet David that was etched in my memory from my mother's story instantly came to mind. As a child, when my mother was telling me a story, I would dramatize it in my mind. I would visualize the characters' features based on the vivid descriptions in the way she told the story.

I met Hanafi, without knowing that he was the brother of my mother's best friend, in the summer of 1973. It was dark when I saw him, around 3:00 a.m., at Manises Airport in Valencia. As we were descending the steps of the plane, one of the kids behind me, who apparently knew Hanafi very well, hollered a greeting at him: "Hello, hello, Hanafi!" Hanafi was waiting for us by the steps with other Saharawi youth leaders in the General Government of what was then the Spanish Sahara. He came up to us kids as we filed down the steps and greeted us one by one. To me, his face seemed like that of the prophet in Mama's story—Dauda. He was dark and tall with a mane of straight black hair, his eyes full of life and tender, with an intense look that made it seem as though they wanted to say something to you.

Detu's story about the prophet appears in many passages of the Qur'an. From what I heard her say on several occasions, the prophet David was the most handsome of all men since the creation of the universe. Legend has it that he once visited a place where some women were weaving and cutting fabrics with very sharp scissors. When the women saw him, they became overwhelmed and smitten by how handsome he was, and, instead of cutting the fabrics, they cut their hands without realizing what they were doing and without feeling the pain of their injuries. His good looks were unparalleled, according to the stories in some old books in Arabic.

My Mother's Other Close Friends

Mama had so many male and female friends in her lifetime. So many people remember her and her neighborliness in the old days when they lived on the plains and in the fields and valleys of Tiris and among the soft, fine, white sand dunes of Legreiaa or Elb Um Duellat.

She lives on in those lovely places in southern Tiris—places such as the hills of Auserd, Leglat, Derraman, Wankarat, Gleybat Legleya, Bu Lariah—where she used to camp with her *frig* of family members and friends. These places, and many other parts of the land, have missed her all these years, from the time she became a refugee until her passing.

She had many female friends, but the ones that she remembered the most and spoke about most often were Mariam Mohamed Chej; El Bagra Mint El Kenti and her mother, Gali Mint Edaf; Lamat Mint Hammada; Heimu Mint Farachi; Mneimunat Mint Ahmed Lali; and Treibi Mint El Kori. The latter's son, Sidahmed Barray, was a great school friend of mine, with whom I also used to go hiking in the mountains of Auserd. I ran into him again in the 1980s when he had become a well-known young military leader, and I saw him fall in combat on August 8, 1987, in the battle of Gleib Teralalal, near Auserd. Many of those friends of my mother's are no longer with us.

She and my father also had many great friends, such as Agmeini Uld Nayem, the friend who introduced them, and Aglaminhum Uld Labeidi, Boiba Uld Edaf, Chejuna Uld Mulay Ali, and his siblings Gah and Sidahmed. I have also known the *Ahel* Sueilim Uld Ahmed Lebrahim family from a very young age, and I remember them as great friends of hers and also of my father's. I thought very highly of that family, who, according to my sister Aichanana, were our neighbors for many years. There was also the family of Dua Uld Ergueibi and his siblings, who have all passed away within these last few years while living in exile. And the list goes on. I should not forget El Fadel Uld Sidi Alal, Humid Uld Ahmed Uld

Hmeimid, or Mohamed Abdelahe Uld El Galaui, who was a well-known judge and a poet in the 1970s in Western Sahara. One of his children, by the way, was my friend at school in both the Sahara and Cuba. He's a friend whom I value greatly, especially because I came to have a closer relationship with him during our time as students in exile. He had a scholarly and cultured air about him, like his father, Mohamed Abdelahe. Mohamed Uld Noucha was another great friend of my parents'; he lived for a while in our house in Auserd in the 1970s when he was doing military service in our town along with my father.

My mother also made a lot of friends during her later years in the refugee camps. However, I wanted to follow the trail of the memories of her as a young woman in the Sahara, which is where I have the most recollections of her, of her youth, and of our childhood. Being very young and strong at that time, she spent those years of her life simply enjoying us.

By the time she had my oldest sister in 1958, Mama was already quite mature. Her intelligence and good manners were an inspiration to the people who met her, and she was even cited as an example of an intelligent woman who was loved by those around her.

By continuing to talk about her friends, I am pleasing her; I am following her good advice; I am simply expressing my gratitude to others as she often encouraged us to do, saying, "We must remember our friends. We must not forget them, because they are the brothers and sisters who were right there with us when we needed them."

These friends, whom I have tried to look for or to remember, as she always advised us to do, take me back to her life in another era. They are a missing link in my childhood, because each of their faces tells me that they carry Mama within them.

I have seen some of her friends during these years in which we have been in exile—now all gray-haired and exhausted because of the long wait—yearning to breathe, once again, the air that sustained them for so many years, somewhere in the Sahara. Many of them have become frail from the ravages of living for so long in the worst desert that we have ever known during these more than thirty years of banishment from our home.

III.

THE ENCOUNTER IN ABOILAY LEYUAD:
OUR YEARS IN THE SAHARA

In 1956 the *Ahel* Omar Ali Uld Embarek Fal—Mama's
family—were leading their nomadic life in the Aboilay
Leyuad area, forty kilometers northeast of Auserd. By
then, Detu was sixteen years old. My father was an
eighteen-year-old young man who was doing his military
service with the Nomad Troops, the equivalent of special
troops. It was a regiment that was created by Spain in the
1930s and was also known in the Sahara as *lharca* or
"partisanos."[i]

Auserd is about fifty kilometers from the valley of
Aboilay, and my father already knew my mother's family,
so when he found out that they had recently set up camp
there, he asked for a few days of leave to go and see them
with his friend Agmeini Uld Nayem. I had asked Detu, a
month before she left us, and she told me the story of
where and how she and my father had met.

My father then formally asked for her hand in mar-
riage in the presence of his best friend and intermediary,

---

i. In this context, "partisanos" refers to insurgents who resisted the colonial presence in their land.

and a few months later, they would marry in the town of Dumsia, which is located on the northern border of Tiris with Zemur Labiad. From then on, my parents lived happily together, moving between Auserd and the different towns in Tiris.

We all grew up together, my siblings and I, in the bosom of a humble and close-knit family. Mama was in charge of all our education from the time we were very little, and she taught us to read and write our first letters of the alphabet. Furthermore, she enrolled us in the first schools that were set up in Auserd in the 1960s, a privilege that few children in our area had because of their families' nomadic lifestyle.

Whenever the valleys in the town turned green and fresh, people's nomadic instincts would be awakened and they would leave their houses behind and enjoy a few months of camping at a *uad*, a *grara*, or a valley in Tiris.

They would buy some goats or sheep for milk and for making *edhen* and *zibda*, exquisite kinds of butter made from the milk of camels or sheep. The return to nomadic life was beneficial to families in several ways, although it was also inconvenient in that the children had to give up school for the duration of the nomadic season. Mama would often find a way of sending us to school so that we did not miss classes. At times we were given a ride by friends who had a car, and at other times I had to find my own way of getting there. Sometimes I had to walk several kilometers with other friends—such as the time when we were camping in the valley of Lmanhar—which meant I had to get up very early to get to school each day, and we would return in the evenings by car with neighbors who worked in town.

My father was away from home often because he had to serve in the patrol unit, guarding the borders, and sometimes he had to go on long missions to other towns, such as Tichla, Agueinit, or Bir Nazaran. In the late 1960s my father requested to be discharged from the army after many years in active service. He set up a small shop that sold honey, which he brought in from Mauritania, and women's cosmetics.

In 1969 it rained a lot all over the territory, especially in Tiris, and my father bought an all-terrain vehicle, a Land Rover Santana, from a friend of his called Humid Uld Ahmed Uld Hmeimid. He decided to leave the city with the family to go and camp with my aunts and uncles in the valleys of Amiskarif, Wankarat, and Amzeili. Mama did not agree with my father, because he had used five of our pack camels, which she valued very much, as part of the payment for the vehicle. At times, when she saw that the vehicle's battery had run down and it had to be push-started, she would weep as she remembered those camels on which she used to travel trouble free with all her household items.

My family spent almost the entire summer there, together with my maternal aunts and uncles. I recall that the area was home to a species of gazelles called *sfara*. Several herds grazed in the valleys, and at night they would climb up the hills to seek refuge from the foxes and wolves. My father and my uncles would sometimes hunt the gazelles by chasing them down with his vehicle, and they would distribute the meat among family and neighbors. Their meat is a Saharawi delicacy, and they were protected during the colonial era, although they were hunted indiscriminately by the Nomad Troops who patrolled the territory's borders.

My Uncle Moulud

I sometimes heard my uncle Moulud, my mother's brother, tell stories about his abysmal failures at hunting during the expeditions that he organized—he was really terrible at hunting. My father and Mohamed, one of my other uncles, often laughed at Moulud and called him "the disastrous hunter." My uncle had a short-range weapon, so he had to get very close to his target to take it down, which is why more often than not, he would be detected by the animals.

Moulud is quite the character in our family. We all consider him to be very intelligent, and he is always the protagonist of all kinds of stories and anecdotes. He has his own philosophy on life, and he would use his ideas to explain anything that happened to him in his work as a herder, a hunter, a *deyar*, a well digger, or a camel trainer. He frequently pulled scary pranks on his siblings, his acquaintances, and my father, who is still terrified of his unpredictable mischief.

Mama would often tell me stories about Moulud, some of the many stories in which her brother was the central figure. One that really shows my uncle's personality is the story about how he and his friends made their way one night to the venue of the festivities for a wedding that was taking place near their *frig*. Traditionally, wedding celebrations were a weeklong affair. During the week of the wedding, it is customary for Saharawis to have camel races and play a Saharawi bowling game, *um talbat*, *araah*, a game of *dabus*, or to have a shooting competition called *shara*. And at night, they enjoy music, dancing, and lavish meals, mostly grilled camel meat—a delicacy among Saharawi desert nomads—along with the traditional couscous.

Now, back to the story of Moulud. On the night of the wedding, he plotted to make off with two halves of a camel that had been prepared for the banquet in honor of the guests. He and his group of friends hid near the *zriba*. At that time of night, the family's livestock were resting, lying down in the *barracado* position and chewing the cud that they had stored in their voluminous stomachs from their day of grazing. Under cover of darkness, Moulud took his chance when the organizers got distracted. He raided the kitchen, making off with a whole lamb, while his friends grabbed various parts of the grilled camel meat. One of the organizers realized what had happened and raised the alarm. Several men took off chasing after the prankster bandits of the *frig*.

Without missing a beat, Moulud jumped onto an old, tame female camel that was resting, got her to stand, climbed onto her back, and remained still. Because it was dark, none of the wedding organizers saw him or thought anything of the camel standing up, and my uncle sat there, atop the camel, eating the lamb until he saw his friends' pursuers returning empty-handed. At that moment he felt safe, jumped off the camel, and headed in the direction that the others had fled. I heard this story directly from my mother's lips on more than one occasion when she and her friends were talking about the famous stories of the unsuccessful hunter, my uncle Moulud.

My Aversion to Greasy Food

Mama found her brother's pranks very funny, and she and her family and friends enjoyed talking about them. When she wasn't going through a rough time from her asthma attacks, she would have a good time with us and our antics. She knew each one of her children perfectly well, and she enjoyed our little stories and childish blunders.

According to my mother, from a very young age, I found animal fat and animal fat derivatives, such as suet, lard, and butter, absolutely repulsive, and I particularly disliked their smell. Once when I became extremely congested, she got very worried because she knew that I was not going to take kindly to the traditional remedy for my condition, and so she grabbed me by force and put a few drops of warm *edhen* into my nostrils to ease the congestion. It is an effective traditional remedy that is still used in the *badia* as an analgesic. My mother really believed in its efficacy, but I on the other hand found it terribly disgusting. When she let go of me, I ran away from her, rubbing myself as hard as I could in an attempt to get rid of that horrible smell.

Detu maintained that I had never used obscene or insulting language with her, but that day, I furiously said to her, "Mama, I promise you that I will get some urine one day and wait until you fall asleep, and then I will pour it down your nose just as you poured that disgusting oil down mine!"

She found the story funny, and even when I had become an adult, she would bring it up at the nightly family gatherings over tea, when she was telling stories about each one of us and our childhood silliness and missteps. As a grown man, I said to her, "Mama, can you forgive me for what I said? I feel really remorseful."

She laughed and said that she did not remember anything that suggested that I had ever behaved badly toward her.

She ended by saying, "There is nothing to be sorry for, you have never offended me."

Memories of Our Home in Auserd

My last telephone conversation with her took place one October night in 2006. I asked her, "Mama, where would you love to be camping right now, with your *jaima* and some Tirisian *shuail*? In some place in Tiris, right?"

And without hesitating or even thinking about it, she said with her usual sweet smile, "Do you know where? On the slopes of Galb Ashalay."

I laughed for a while and answered, "What a lovely place you have chosen, Mama."

"But surely, Galb Ashalay is in the liberated territories, or did it end up behind the wall that the Moroccans built?"

"Mama, you've got to ask Badi the poet, because he has a poem dedicated to Galb Ashalay."

I then explained to her that Galb Ashalay was on the occupied side and that it broke my heart, because the occupiers do not know what a hill in Tiris, such as Galb Ashalay and its dune, means to a Saharawi.

She told me that we lived there in the 1970s and that we had a good year. It rained a lot, and the whole territory was green and teeming with the camels and *jaimas* of family and friends. There was so much prosperity for everyone; it was unforgettable. In the end, I assured her that one day we would go back to visit and to camp in those *mirhan* of the old days.

Forever the optimist, I never saw Mama give up because of how difficult our situation was or because of the unpredictable challenges that she faced. I think I inherited her optimism, which is what helped me hold on for the eleven years when I was in exile, far away and separated from her.

I remember that my uncle Mohamed Fadel, Boiba, had written a lovely poem by a pre-Islamic Arabic poet on one of the walls of our house in Auserd, which said:

ولا يغــــدر بصاحبك الزمان   إلا يا دار لا يدخــــــلك حزن

إذا ما ضاق بالضيف المكان   فنعــم الدار تأوي كل ضيــف

Oh, my house,
in you,
let there be no hiding place for sorrow,
and let not the bad times destroy you.
A home is a blessing
for protecting the guest
who is in distress.

The poem was written on the wall by my uncle Boiba in beautiful Arabic script inside a geometric frame similar to the ones that are typically used to decorate traditional Bedouin leather handicrafts. Mama used to say that when she read that poem it made her feel that our house would provide refuge and shelter for whomever needed it. There was another poem about good hospitality written on the wall, but I no longer remember it.

I left our house in the fall of 1975, and I would only see it again eleven years later, one month before Auserd fell into the hands of the Moroccan army. My town had previously been occupied by Mauritania from 1976 to 1979. I was fortunate to see our house in the summer of 1986 in the company of my uncle Boiba. I was moved when I saw those walls within which I had spent my childhood, walls that were now destroyed by the war. I tried to look among the rubble for the wall with that poem, but everything was in ruins.

"Be very careful," my uncle cautioned me, "there are still live grenades, antipersonnel mines, and mortar shells that were left here by the Mauritanian and Moroccan soldiers. We can't look around anymore. This is what the invaders have left us, ruins and more ruins."

Right across from our house, we found the rubble of what had been the house of my teacher Mohamed Abdalehi Uld Beddi and what had been the houses of other Auserd families, such as *Ahel* Nayem Uld Ahmed Laali and *Ahel* Esahil. The houses of El Galb Uld Ahmed Zein, Boiba Uld Eddaf, Mohamed Abdelahi El Galaui, and many others were also in ruins. All those houses were once the homes of neighbors whom I remember very well from my childhood.

My Father's Absence

When my father was in the army, he would always manage to find other work to supplement our family's income. In his business ventures, he always relied on my mother, about whom he reminisced, saying she was "the most intelligent woman that I had ever known, my support during the three decades that we were together. Sometimes I would ignore her advice, but I would ultimately take it, because she was always reasonable, realistic, and incredibly insightful."

In late 1969 my father traveled to Zouérat, a Mauritanian town on the border with Western Sahara, to purchase some merchandise for our shop. On the way, as he was resting in some Saharawi *jaimas*, two individuals showed up asking for help to tow their car, which had broken down nearby. My father, with the best of intentions and without hesitating, sent his driver to go with them in his car while he waited in his hosts' *jaimas*.

It turned out that it was all really an orchestrated ploy to steal the vehicle because of some outstanding debts between the first owner of the car and those individuals. My father, however, had purchased the car from a second owner, who, like him, had absolutely nothing to do with that debt. Dad went off to El-Aaiún to report the theft of his car. He had to file a complaint against the perpetrators of the crime and also against the previous owners, who were all summoned by the court in that city.

The trial took several months, and the week right after he had won the case, he got ready to leave El-Aaiún, having been away from home for so long. That very day— June 17, 1970—was when the first Saharawi uprising against Spain, to demand social reforms for our people, broke out. Those incidents, which came to be known as the Zemla or the Barrio de Piedra uprising, led to the death of many Saharawi demonstrators and to the disappearance of the original mastermind behind the Saharawi national liberation movement, the journalist Sidi Brahim Basiri, who has never been heard from since. The Legion[8] mounted a ferocious attack against the insurgents—leaving many fatalities in its wake—and the city was cut off from the rest of the territory. My father was unable to leave, and he had to wait for several weeks before he could travel. He would later recount that the governor of Auserd, with whom he had worked for many years, was serving in El-Aaiún at the time and that he was the one who had issued a document to my father that enabled him to leave without running into any problems at the roadblocks that had been set up by the Legion.

We were all little at the time and spent that year with my mother and our uncles and aunts in the *badia*. We were unable to go to school, although my mother always kept up with giving us our lessons on a *louh*. She took charge of keeping our family safe, and she did everything, from tending our camels to managing and rationing our provisions in order to keep us fed. She protected and took care of all of us, with the help of her brothers Moulud, Mohamed, and Boiba. Whenever he was able to do so, my father sent us money, clothes, and provisions.

---

8. The Legion (La Legión Española or La Legión, in Spanish) is a unit of the Spanish Armed Forces.

The very first tape recorder that I saw, a Philips, was sent to us by my father through some friends. He sent one to my mother and others as gifts to my aunts. I must admit that those devices aroused an insatiable curiosity in me for a very long time. I would look at them over and over again, checking to see where the voices were coming from and trying to figure out where the singers and the people who were talking were hiding and how they could be so small as to fit into that tiny space—a receiver in a lovely brown leather case, with an adjustable strap for carrying it around.

Mama understood my astonishment, and she would watch and laugh at my dogged efforts to find the singers inside the tape recorder. But she left me to figure it out on my own, to find an explanation by reasoning and to arrive at the logical conclusion that it was not possible to have living beings inside the device.

When Mama invited her sisters or friends over for tea, she would bring out the radio when they were chatting or resting. In those days, there were four of us siblings, my older sister, my brother who comes after me, a sister who comes after him, and me. According to her siblings, Detu could single-handedly take care of any emergencies that arose at the *badia*, on behalf of her family and of others. Whenever one of those sudden windstorms started pounding the desert, she would adjust her *jaima* to keep it intact by tautening the main ropes and loosening the secondary ones, keep us children sheltered in a safe place, and then go out to help other camp residents whose *jaimas* were flapping in the wind or even collapsing on top of them.

She knew how to milk camels, hold them down, dispatch them in the morning along with her siblings' herd, separate them from the rest of the herd at night, and corral them next to our *jaima* to milk them for the family. She was not a big woman. She was quite slender, tall, and very nimble, and she did not gain weight easily, although that plump physique did appeal to her when she was very young. In later years she came to understand the health issues associated with obesity, so she took very good care of herself so as not to put on weight.

She always ate with us from the same plate. She would share out the meat in small pieces, "so that you don't choke on it," she would say to us. She used to say that it was bad manners to eat excessively, and she disliked seeing people eat ravenously, because it made the food look unsavory. It was a good trait that I picked up from her when I was a child.

She used to tell us about a man who once came to visit us from Mauritania, a gluttonous fellow who devoured his food. Right from the day I first saw him I said, "Mama, I am not going to eat here as long as this gentleman is in our house. The way he eats is disgusting." In our society it is considered rude to talk about food, and it is not common practice among Saharawis, because there are always more relevant issues that ought to engage and preoccupy intelligent minds.

According to Mama, I did not eat even once in our house the entire time that the man was there, and I would go and eat with my aunts to avoid seeing the greedy gentleman. She would often have a good laugh at my reactions, and she was very amused by the way I was put off by our guest.

My mother was such a good person that she always kept her feelings of displeasure or discomfort to herself. She was discreet about other people's flaws, and she detested the rumors and gossip circulated by boastful people. She was brilliant and charming in the way that she interacted with others. Her friends were always extremely well-mannered people from whom she learned even more and through whom she enriched her knowledge.

I remember countless stories as a child with Mama. She often reminded me that nothing had ever frightened me, not even the stories about the night monster that my grandfather used to tell me, and not even the desert animals such as *edabaa*, the dangerous desert hyenas who in Saharawi lore were said to cast a spell on you and carry you off to their lairs.

Because I was fearless, I would hide underneath some large earthenware jars at night and frighten my aunts by making strange noises and playing tricks on them. Once, when I was eight years old, my parents' friends dared me to go and place a lamp on top of some tombs in a cemetery. They thought I wouldn't be able to do it, but to me it was all a joke, and the cemetery inspired no sense of danger or awe in me.

It was nighttime, so they gave me the lamp. My mother had stepped out to do something in the kitchen, so she was unaware of the challenge and thought that I was up to one of my little pranks for fun and that was all. I left the *jaima* without her knowledge and headed for the cemetery, which was located right on the side of a small hill. When I got there, I placed the lamp smack on top of a tomb, turning it to face in the direction from which I had come, and headed back.

However, on my way back, seeing that I was not scared, some people hid along the way, brushing the ground with some branches behind me. But that didn't startle me either. To me, those things weren't harmful, since I didn't have a negative mindset.

My mother found out what was happening because all my friends were following me, laughing. Hamad-da Uld Daf, who fell in the war, said to my mother, "You'll have yourself an interesting man in the future."

She responded that my grandfather Hamadi had told her something similar. My grandfather affectionately called me *ljruf*—little lamb—a name that was given to people who were thought to bring good luck and who were always accompanied by *baraka*. My paternal grandfather looked at me and said to Jadiyetu, "You'll see that this funny little kid will one day become the son that the family depends on."

I consulted my older sister on some questions that I had about Mama; it was during one of my trips back to the camps to visit my family after Detu had left us. There were so many things that I had wanted to ask my mother about when I visited her for the last time during Holy Week in 2006. However, Detu was in no condition to answer the list of questions that I had prepared in my planner. I wanted to talk to her about poetry and authors, and I wanted to ask her about my childhood, my escape as a result of the decision that she took, her thoughts about me during those years when I was gone, and I also had questions about her best friends, whom I had met when I was a child. In short, I had a lot to talk to Mama about. I devoted that week of our visit entirely to her; however, it was due to other matters that had little to do with poetry, stories, and reminiscing. We had to take her to the hospital for a complete run of tests and for the fluids that were being retained by her weary body to be drained. The fact of the matter is that, a month later, she was feeling much better. I called her every week, and she was able to answer all my outstanding questions on the phone.

My sister told me that, regarding my flight that moonlit night so long ago in 1975, when my mother made the decision to prepare for me to flee, she chanted some verses behind me to ensure that no ill would befall me. My sister Nana would often say that Mama was prescient. She could sense a good omen, and in every situation, she followed her intuition with utmost optimism, always trusting that everything would turn out well.

She said that she had taken that decision because she realized that it would open up new opportunities for me. It made her feel relieved to know that I wasn't going to end up like many of the other young men who became spies for the occupying military forces out of economic necessity or just became aimless kids with no future or prospects. She never expressed any regret about her decision when she spoke about me to family, friends, or neighbors who might have criticized her for the action that she had taken: "But how could you have let your son escape all by himself in the middle of a war, unprotected by anyone?"

I remember that, during my flight, I ran into a friend, a wonderful young man in my age group and a native of

Auserd, who parted company with me just as we arrived at a Saharawi army base in Gleybat Legleya. If my memory serves me right, he had run into a family member who was also on his way into exile and had joined him. I never heard from him again until we met eleven years later. My friend, Mohamed Fadel Nayum, had studied telecommunications, which is why we crossed paths again and worked together in the 1980s.

The Gatherings and Deylul, the Wise One

My mother would invariably begin every conversation with a famous saying by a Saharawi sage. There is one saying that I learned from her that she would cite in discussions on a historical topic that, from her point of view, one ought to be very knowledgeable about. She would say, "You have to be as infallible as the words of Deylul, otherwise people will not listen to you." My mother recounted many stories about Deylul. She considered him to be a role model because of his larger-than-life and self-assured personality, which made him very famous among the inhabitants of the territory.

My mother maintained that Deylul was a wise man because he knew everything about nomadic people and their environment. She used to say that he could forecast the weather by observing the changes and abnormalities in the behavior of camels and other animals. For all those reasons, he was an authority on climatological changes among the nomads in the region. His pronouncements were irrefutable; he was a born survivor of the natural inclement weather of the desert because of his deep knowledge of how to handle the physical environment around him.

I was fortunate to meet one of his grandchildren and to travel with him on a long journey to Tiris in the 1980s. At first I didn't know who he was, but I observed how he took part in the conversations and his pleasant attitude toward other people. And one day I asked him point-blank, "Your name is Uld Deylul. Are you the son of the famous Deylul, or is it just a coincidence that you share the same last name?" And before he could respond, I added, "Do you know why I'm asking? I've watched you speaking many times, you're always very sure of what you say, and to my knowledge your words haven't been disproved or questioned by anyone. All our friends speak well of you, and that's why I'm asking if you are the son of our Deylul."

He asked me how I knew Deylul, and I explained to him that I had heard my mother speak of that famous man ever since I was a child and that whenever she questioned the credibility of someone's information, she would say, "It lacks the certainty of Uld Deylul's words." After a pleasant conversation, the man admitted that he was the grandson of the Saharawi sage Deylul. Then I said to him, "You have certainly inherited a number of your grandfather's admirable qualities." He responded, smiling, "Our generation reminds me of that proverb that says, 'The great camel rises up and leaves behind his excrement.' We will never be as good as our grandparents were, I wish it were not the case."

I recall that when I returned to the Saharawi refugee camps in Algeria, I told Mama how I had met Deylul's grandson, and she looked at me as if she were searching in her memory for some story about his descendants. "I don't know anyone from that family, but I think I have heard of close family members of Deylul's who lived between the borders of the eastern part of Tiris and Mauritania." And she continued: "Deylul knew the name of every plant that lives and dies in the Sahara. He named all the seasons of the desert, he forecast the changes in the weather. He will forever be remembered for his rigor in the way he saw and said things."

The Story of How My Grandfather Omar Almost Starved to Death

Detu would often tell us the fascinating story of what happened to her father in the desert. My maternal grandfather Omar, who passed away in 1959, as my uncle Mohamed Moulud used to remind us, once got lost in the middle of a terrible windstorm that separated him from his family and his herd of camels, and he survived. It happened while they were traveling in a caravan to an area that had a lot of grass for the animals and good wells, with plans of setting up camp there. This is his story, one in which my grandfather and, indeed, his whole family were really pushed to the brink and forced to put into practice their ancestral knowledge of how to survive in the desert.

One day, when my mother was little, my grandparents decided to gather their herd and move to the southern region of the territory in search of grazing land and water. During the night, they readied the camels that carried their personal effects, and they fed their six children. They took down their *jaima* and then proceeded to load their belongings onto their *emrakib*.

The camels were upset because their period of rest in *lemrah*, after a long day of grazing, had been interrupted. In a confused hubbub of cries, nervous mothers and kids were searching for one another in the darkness, and my grandfather was shouting, "Ohh, ohh, ohh," the sound that was used to calm down the animals. The *emrakib*, which were not with the rest of the camels, were lying in front of the *jaima*, each one of them with their *jzama* attached to a silver ring on the upper part of their flared nostrils, ruminating calmly while the first pack saddles were being placed on their backs.

Nisha, my grandmother, was placing and fastening her *amshakab* on Zeirig, her favorite camel, with the help of my uncles Lajdar and Alati, the oldest of the children, who was thirteen at the time. Meanwhile, Omar was trying to finish loading the bulk of their belongings onto the three pack camels, Sheil, Lehmami, and the powerful Arumay, who always carried the larger loads, such as the *jaima*, its sheets, and all the *ercaiz*. Arumay was a robust dark brown male with shaggy shoulders and powerful legs, an animal who was very elegant and obedient, thanks to his expert trainer, my grandfather. My grandmother loved it when he bellowed, saying that he was a loyal animal even during the rutting season when male camels go through hormonal changes because of their condition and fight with their owners to be free and alone with the females.

My grandfather Omar knew that grazing land was abundant in the southern region and that it was the best place for his family and *ibil*. In the desert, news—*lajabar*—travels by word of mouth among the herders and *deyarin*. He had gathered enough information through his seasonal migration with his livestock and his encounters, along the way, with Bedouins, who were always on the lookout for places where there had been rain.

The weather and the cover of darkness were the two elements that my grandparents were waiting for in order to cover several kilometers and arrive by daybreak at a place that was likely to offer them the absolute peace and tranquility of nomadic life. Everything was ready that night, and the livestock were walking southward, where, with any luck, my grandparents hoped to quickly set up camp within a week.

Omar was not familiar with the place where they were headed, and on the third day, at dawn, they were hit by an unprecedented windstorm with blowing winds from the south, which made it impossible for even a desert man weathered by that hostile environment to see beyond his outstretched arm. My grandmother was screaming at Omar to remain with the group and to not go after any of the straggling livestock. He was quickly going back and forth, trying to keep the herd together and prevent the young camels from wandering off, as they were trailing behind because they couldn't keep up with the adult ones.

Suddenly, the dark silhouette of Omar riding on the back of Elbeyed disappeared from my grandmother's view, and although she tried to locate him at the farthest end of the herd, she couldn't see him or hear Elbeyed's gentle bellowing. She called out, "Omar, Omar, Omar, where are you?!," and repeated over and over again, "*Ina lilahi! Ina lilahi!*," that visceral cry of pain, sadness, and helplessness at the drama that was unfolding around her.

The oldest of the children, who was riding next to her in the *amshakab*, kept asking, "Mama, where is Father? I can't hear him calling the animals." Nisha prudently replied that he had stayed behind to look for a straggling *huar*, and she tried to calm him down, telling him not to worry and that his father would soon catch up with them. She continued to stay with the herd and worked vigorously to keep everything together and on the move. From time to time, she would say "esh, esh, esh" to prevent the animals from scattering and to make them keep the pace, all huddled together, and moving in the same direction.

The wind was getting stronger and stronger, and the children were crying because it was time to set up camp and for them to have their meal of milk or *kisra*, if possible. Stunned by the weather conditions and the disappearance of her husband, she drew strength from the innermost core of her Bedouin identity and forged ahead, because she knew that if she stopped, even for a second, everything would fall apart, and she absolutely did not want to lose the animals that were carrying the water on their backs, and so she decided to keep going until the storm died down.

Omar had gone in a completely unfamiliar direction, and seeing that he had lost his bearings, he stopped for a moment and went toward some shrubs to find out if they bore any signs that would guide him. However, the wind had destroyed all the signs. The tops of the shrubs were bent in another direction, and the sand that gathered in the crooks of the branches of every shrub and always indicated the way south had disappeared. The sun was invisible, and all was darkness around him. Omar's experience and the fifty years that he had lived in the harsh desert environment were of no use to him at all in that sudden onslaught from nature. He knew that it was indomitable and that it was simply the will of God.

He wandered nonstop on his camel that whole day, searching for tracks and animal dung and listening for bellowing, the whimpering of children, or his wife's voice. He called out to Arumay many times, hoping to be guided by the camel's response, and he let his Elbeyed run free until well into the night the following day, in case his instincts led him to the rest of the herd. But he couldn't find any traces, and meanwhile the wind raged on unabated. Omar was exhausted, and his camel needed to graze and regain his strength to keep going.

Disconcerted by the situation of his wife and children, Omar thought about the water and the provisions that they were carrying on the humps of the camels and wondered how Nisha and the children would be able to reach them. He looked at the opaque sky, convinced that God was everywhere, as he had learned as a very small child from his father, and exclaimed in a conciliatory tone, as if he were praying, "Dear God, now I really leave Nisha, Alati, Jadiyetu, Lajdar, Yeslem, Moulud, and Jueya in your hands! You would know where they are! You will take care of them! Guide the instincts that you gave me at the age of five when I looked after my family's small herd! The drought is driving me out and evicting me from my land, and hunger is devouring the bellies of my children, my wife, and my camels. Stand by me at this crucial moment!"

He had gone several hours without eating or drinking, as all the provisions had remained on Lehmami's back, and the water and a few sacks of barley were hidden in Nisha's *tezaya*. Helped by the cool winter weather, which was working in his favor, Omar had not felt thirsty during that time. However, he had begun to feel the first symptoms of going without food for two days, and his knees buckled when he climbed down from his camel to gather some wild plants for food. He found very few plants, and they hardly provided him with any nourishment.

When it was time for one of the five daily prayers, Omar would cast his eyes over the terrain from his perch atop Elbeyed, looking for a place that had a little bit of foliage to give his camel a break, while he performed the rituals that were required of him as a believer. Since he couldn't see the sun, he calculated the time by watching certain behaviors in Elbeyed, and if it was already nightfall, the animal would bellow gently and walk more slowly to indicate his need to rest. Omar would then order him to stop, and he would climb down from his *rahla*. Then he would look for an acacia or any other shrub to protect himself from the horrendous *guetma*.

That night, the two of them rested, protected by the crown of a *talha* that had been uprooted by the wind. It was the best gift from nature after three days of going without food. There were still a few *jarrub* on the branches, which had otherwise been stripped bare by the wind. Elbeyed ate all the tender parts of the crown, and Omar collected the few pods of *jarrub* and began to chew them slowly, but they were bitter because they were not yet dry.

As he thought about his family, Omar felt a sense of calm because he had always had an unwavering faith in his wife, especially during tough times or when they had to make life-and-death decisions. He again said a prayer for everyone's safety. When he finished praying, he tethered his camel firmly and tied the reins together securely. Leaning his back into Elbeyed's shoulders to shield himself from the cold and the winds, he spent the whole night curled up with his stomach rumbling ceaselessly.

The animal shook his head because of the dust that had accumulated on his body. My grandfather understood at once the unmistakable sign that Elbeyed had given. Another day with the windstorm raging on, another day of hunger and thirst, another day for a man of the desert thrown off course by the force of nature and its rigors. Omar was a tall and thin man, with a penetrating gaze, an aquiline nose, high cheekbones, and dark, curly hair. The camel was weakening fast, after several weeks of being on the move with the family, with no food and hardly any rest. My grandfather remembered what he had been taught to do in those situations—remain calm and stay put until the weather cleared up, the principle for survival among the men of the desert. Luck was not on his side though; he was in an area with little vegetation, which was also unfamiliar to him. He tried to figure out where he was by collecting some stones and the dried roots of some plants. He wanted to examine them carefully to identify the geography of the area, but he could not focus, because he was starving, his legs were trembling, and his vision was clouded by dehydration.

He got up and dragged a few branches of the acacia that had been protecting them toward his camel, and Elbeyed devoured the green, thorny branches with strong bites. Omar remembered that there could be some moisture in the acacia roots, so he looked, and with some difficulty he pulled out some roots that still contained a very sweet sap and began to chew them. His stomach began to feel better after the severe pain that he had suffered from eating the bitter pods the previous night.

Nisha and their six children had been traveling southward for six days. She had her bearings and was absolutely in control of the situation, although she struggled to load and unload the water tanks that were mounted on Lehmami's saddle when they had to camp or set off again.

By the following day, Omar had completely exhausted his strength and was hallucinating and felt nauseous, but he needed to survive at all costs. He loved his riding camel, Elbeyed, an animal that he had chosen and trained himself. Elbeyed had various tempos to his trot, thanks to his well-developed and hairy tail and his well-proportioned physique. He was a gem of an *azzal*, a camel that had been castrated to enable him to travel many kilometers and withstand hunger and thirst. That is why my grandfather's inevitable decision pained him so much.

Despite his weakness, Omar dug out a hole about half an arm's length deep, put some stones around it, and filled it with some dry kindling sticks that he collected from around the *talha*. From the pocket of his *darraa*, he took out a small iron bar that had been specially treated to produce sparks when it was rubbed against a flint. He placed a fine cotton wick on top of the flint and rubbed the little bar against it two or three times until the sparks ignited the cotton wick, then placed it gently among the thin kindling sticks. The fire began to give off smoke and heat. Omar took out a sharp *mus bleida* from the belt of his pants and stuck its thin blade into the campfire.

At that moment, he knew deep inside how much he and his camel needed each other in that extreme situation. Without pausing to think, he sliced off Elbeyed's tail in one go with the practically red-hot knife, immediately using the same blade to cauterize the wound to prevent hemorrhaging. He then found a plant with healing properties, chewed its leaves, and applied them to the two phalanges that remained of Elbeyed's tail. After that, Omar stroked his head and kissed the nape of his neck several times, saying to him, "You and I have no choice but to gather strength to go and look for our family."

That night, Omar ate meat, and with that and the moist acacia roots, he regained some energy to keep going. The following day, he decided to continue traveling against the wind, given that its direction had not changed since the first day; the wind was blowing from the south, and he headed in that direction. Every time he came across any patch of green grass, he would stop and allow Elbeyed to replenish his energy. After eight days of travel at a camel's pace, he saw droppings that had been left behind by an encampment of animals and stopped to carefully examine those signs of life. He determined that his family had camped there approximately a week earlier, based on the number of marks that each camel had made and the moisture level in the animals' dung.

Omar survived ten more days on the rest of his camel's tail and the roots that he found. By the second week, the weather had begun to clear up, and there had been some rain that had left puddles of water, from which Omar and his Elbeyed drank. My grandfather had begun to find his bearings and to come across herders and *deyarin*, with whom he exchanged information about his family and the damage caused by *Am el guetma*, "the year of the windstorm," as Saharawis came to call that year.

That night, while Nisha was milking the camels for supper next to the campfire of their *jaima* with the help of the oldest of her little children, she heard Elbeyed's melancholic bellow as he knelt down in the sand. Omar climbed down from his back and called out to his wife and children, "Are you all okay?" The little ones emerged from the *jaima* and flew into his arms. Nisha, emotional at the sight of the state her husband was in, went to him with a bowl of fresh milk and offered it to him, saying, "Drink this first." She asked the children to let go of him so that he could drink it. From that night onward, Elbeyed was no longer called by that name, and he instead

65

became Guilal because of his sliced-off tail. My grandfather did not starve to death, thanks to his camel's tail, and he and Nisha used his heroic story to teach us all a lesson on not giving up in the face of adversity.

This story, which could pass as fiction, really happened, as we in my family know very well. I heard it from the lips of my mother many times when I was a child, and at the time, I thought it was one of those endearing *Shertat* tales, but it's all true, and it really happened, and that is how it continued to be told to me on many occasions as an adult.

The Abduction of My Grandfather Hamadi

Regarding the North, I remember a story that I used to hear my mother tell about how my paternal grandfather, Hamadi, was abducted when he once traveled to a trading post at the border with Morocco to sell camels to some Moroccans. It turned out that they were the typical criminals that we would often come across at the border. According to Mama, my grandfather said that they tied his hands and put him in a house with five doors that locked behind him.

They left him there with one of the crooks guarding him with a wooden truncheon. But when the guard got distracted, he took advantage of that, broke the restraints on his hands, pounced on the stick, hit the thief on the head with all his might, and broke down all the doors in his way. The other criminals were coming after him just as he was leaping over the last wall, and he shouted, pretending that he was being rescued by a group of Saharawis, "Come quickly, here are the thieves, get them before they get away!"

That was how he succeeded in escaping captivity to join his friends who were looking for him. My mother kept a treasure trove of stories about both families that she enjoyed reminiscing about with us.

Mama's Camels

When Mama was young, she had a riding camel that had been given to her by her older brother, Alati. Traditionally, among the Saharawis of the *badia*, when a girl got married, she was given a castrated riding camel on the day that she was leaving her family. It had to be a camel that was elegant in its bearing, white if possible, and very well trained so that the young woman would be able to handle him easily.

The name of Mama's camel was Arumay. In 1959 one of my father's brothers needed him to flee from the French persecution against the Saharawi national resistance movement that was fighting the incursions of France into the territory. My uncle asked my mother for her camel, and as always, she couldn't say no, especially when his life was at stake. As my father's brother was saddling Arumay to take him away, my mother looked at her camel as if she were losing a part of herself forever. Detu loved that camel very much.

The following year, when I was born, it was discovered that I had a light brown birthmark that looked like a camel lying down, right below my left armpit. My mother explained that when she gave up her camel, she felt extreme sadness and a sensation similar to the cravings that expectant mothers had at the thought of never seeing him again. She scratched her side, right below her left armpit, passing along, to her way of thinking, her "cravings" to the fetus in her womb. Thus, I was born with the image of that majestic camel that saved the life of my uncle Ami Omar, and which to this day is imprinted below my left armpit in memory of Arumay.

I have countless stories about my mother and teacher and the camels that she loved so much. On one occasion, my family was camping in the northern valley of Auserd in the summertime, and that day, my younger brother, myself, and some other boys had been sent out to tend some camels that had to be milked. There were about ten or fifteen of them, and usually they did not stray from the valley, from where our *jaimas* could be seen. However, that day we got distracted jumping from rock to rock and playing among the dunes. Later on, all exhausted, we rested in the shade of an acacia as the sun was setting and the time was approaching to head back to the *frig* with the camels.

When it came time to leave, the other boys got up and took their herds back to their families, but I remained lying underneath the acacia, unable to get up because of a kind of nightmare that had gripped my entire body. I was trying to scream, to move, but I couldn't. When it got dark, the alarm was raised at the camp that I had gone missing. People started searching for me in the area where the other boys said that they had left me behind, without specifying the exact location.

They lit some brushwood and kept calling out my name, hoping that I would be able to see them and find my bearings. But I was in the grip of a nightmare that only allowed me to move my feet in a way that drew a circle, as certain animals do when they are about to die, drawing a complete circle with their feet in their final death throes.

They spent all night searching for me, with my mother on the verge of passing out because she was afraid that I might have been devoured by an animal, perhaps a desert wolf. At daybreak, just as the first rays of the sun were appearing, a wild cat showed up and climbed on top of me. That was what finally enabled me to react, freeing myself from the nightmare. I jumped up and set off running without knowing exactly where I was. The previous day, a camel with a leather flask of water hanging below its *rahla* had been prepared for us, for when we got thirsty. The adults always reminded us that we had the camel at the ready in case anything happened, if we got bitten by a snake or if we suffered any mishap. The camel was very gentle and tame, which is why he was given to us so that he could take us back to the *frig* if we ever ran into any problems. After a few moments of confusion, I saw the camel lying down with the leather flask hanging from his saddle and went up to him and quenched my thirst. I saw a few of my family's camels some two or three kilometers away from where I was, and I made my way toward them. There was my whole family getting ready to organize a search by following my footprints from the day before.

One of my uncles, I don't recall which of them it was, saw me and called out. Everyone started to run toward me as they shouted to my mother, "He's okay, he's okay! Nothing has happened to him!"

I told them, sobbing, that something had gotten on top of me and prevented me from waking up from the siesta that I was taking in the shade of the acacia. The nightmare and that situation recurred many more times, and I would often ask my uncle Boiba to reach out and touch me from time to time whenever he woke up in the middle of the night, just in case, since that was the only way out of that strange paralysis. Mama didn't make too much of that nightmare, and she would say to me, "Don't think of anything scary when you are going to sleep."

She would often say that the most frightening experience of her life was losing me that night. That incident would keep her up at night even years later.

The Loss of Our Camels

Arumay; Güeyrir, the one with his ears cut off; Shgaár; Elhainash; the one called Bu Kafein, because he had been branded with two ﻙ;[ii] and another camel, a white one that did not have a name.

According to my uncles, this white camel did not see very well in one eye, and so they called him *shaif* rather than the word for "one-eyed one," because for nomadic Saharawis, that word was jinxed. These were my mother's family's pack camels for many years. They were the shoulders that they leaned on, and those pack camels saved their lives on numerous occasions, during natural disasters and other scourges in the desert.

For my research on the story of the camels, I did not ignore the stories that I had heard my mother tell about them when I was a child. Their names were just like the

---

ii. The letter *kaf* of the Arabic alphabet. My mother's family branded their herd with a *kaf*, but in this case, the camel was purchased as a calf from another family that branded with a *kaf* and a dash. When my family also branded him on his neck, he became known as "the one with two *kaf*'s."

names of family members to me, and they transported me to my mother's childhood and her youth because owners and their camels all grew up together. They all stood shoulder to shoulder to deal with the most difficult and the most adverse situations, such as the years of drought and extreme heat. For these reasons, our camels are a part of this tribute from a son and pupil to his mother and teacher.

Mohamed Moulud—my uncle, the wise one—tells me stories about my family whenever I go to the Saharawi camps to visit my grandmother, my siblings, my father, and my aunts and uncles. We all invite one another and gather around tea to celebrate the togetherness that has always kept us united. Any topic is a good one to discuss with them at these types of gatherings. The interlocutor must know how to lead them to the topic of interest in order to learn all about the history of the time when they all lived in the Sahara. That's what I do. I always try to steer the conversation onto my family, because I'm very aware of being in the presence of an inexhaustible source of information about the lives of my mother and her family. I'm also very aware that the living conditions in that place of exile, where my aunts and uncles—and thousands of other Saharawi refugees—find themselves, are inhospitable, so whenever we meet, we have to make the most of it. As I redirected one of our conversations, I asked my uncle about that legendary camel called Arumay and about his memories of him and how he died.

And so, he told me that, in 1972, our family suffered an unprecedented drought during their seasonal migration between the regions of Tiris and Zemur. They moved on to Auserd and its *badia*, while Alati, my mother's oldest brother, stayed behind in the region of Tiris as a seasonal herder in charge of their livestock. He went from place to place in search of pastureland and water for the livestock. And with life's ups and downs, the five pack camels went missing, as would often happen in those circumstances. The missing camels included Arumay, the family's famous camel, who had come back to us after helping my uncle Ami Omar escape.

Alati became both *deyar* and herder to find Arumay and the other camels, and while searching for the five camels, he tried to watch over the bulk of the herd that still remained. However, one day, during an expedition in his role as *deyar*, some tracks that appeared to be those of his camels led him down the valley of Galb Elmusha, where immediately his eyes fell upon his family's five camels. They were all dead as a result of the drought. There lay the remains of Arumay, Elhainash, Güeyrir, Shgaár, Bu Kafein, and the one who could not see out of one eye. Alati approached the site of that sad family misfortune, climbed down from his camel, and, one by one,

73

he examined the dead camels, confirming the Bedouin tragedy. Güeyrir was the only one who was still breathing, with his long neck resting on his side, a position that indicated the seriousness of his condition and the imminent fatal outcome. Having checked them all over, he walked a short distance away from them, overcome by extreme sadness, and with his hands on his head he wept uncontrollably over what for him was the end of a way of life and of his nomadic roots. At that moment he made a statement to his dead camels that my family remembers to this very day—"You are my witnesses: you are the last camels that I will ever herd."

That day, feeling sad and dejected, Alati went back to where the rest of his camels were and entrusted them to his younger brother, Mohamed Moulud, to do with as he saw fit. He settled in the urban areas to look for work in the cities of El-Aaiún and Smara[iii] and gave up that nomadic life that he loved so much.

According to Mohamed Moulud, because of the economic situation and the drought, he decided to leave the livestock to roam free until it came time for them to be watered at the wells of Zbeyra, where the livestock habitually went to drink in the summer. Moulud was in charge of the camels from 1972 to 1974, and in the sum-

---

iii. A city founded by the Saharawi sage Chej Malainin.

mer, he would wait for the rest of the herd there, water and release them, select one or two of them, take them to Smara, sell them, and take the money back to his family. He carried on like that until there were no more camels left that had survived the drought. Just like his older brother, Moulud tried to carve out a path for himself in his new way of life, and in later years he joined the ranks of the colonial army, the Nomad Troops.

Mohamed Moulud and the Flags

According to Mohamed Moulud, in 1956 our family was camping in a valley between the hill of Tiznig and Steilit Uld Bugrein. Spain had just begun the construction of a road. The construction site was marked out with some white flags, above which the Spanish flag flew on a pole, as a sign that there was some work being carried out in that area by the army. One day, when he was out tending the livestock, Mohamed Moulud saw those white flags and another one with red and yellow stripes, and he was struck by those pieces of fabric that were invading his space and getting in the way of his camels' freedom. The poles were very high, and he couldn't reach up far enough to get the flags, so he spent a few days lurking around and thinking of how to remove them or burn them up because they obstructed his view of the horizon, which is extremely important for a Bedouin.

He finally decided to go up the poles, so he selected a very tame female camel, climbed onto her back, and got close enough to the flags. He reached out and pulled down the white construction ones first, and then the Spanish flag that was used to indicate work that was being overseen by the army. He left the place, made a *darraa* from the white flags, and wore it. He tore up the red and yellow striped one into strips and braided them into thin ropes, which he planned to use as reins for the necks of the small camel calves. He then casually set fire to whatever was left of the flag.

My aunt recalls that a very good friend of my grandfather's, who was called Deid Uld Futa, was employed at the road construction site. We were camping in that area, where our *jaima* was the only one in the vicinity, and our family friend would often come over to visit us on weekends when he was not working at the construction site. That afternoon, at the end of his workday, Mohamed Moulud brought the livestock back to his family, and as he was getting them to curl up in front of the *jaima* in *lemrah*, my grandfather Omar went up to welcome him, as he had spent the whole day away from home. When Omar caught sight of the fabric that his son was wearing, he asked him where he had gotten it, and my uncle responded that he had found it on some abandoned poles. Omar got angry, and he scolded him, saying, "Spain will come after us because we have offended her by ripping up her flag."

Moulud did not understand the gravity of what he had done, and he was not bothered by the incident. However, my grandfather was a very sensible person who never did anything to offend anyone, and that is how he had raised all his children. What had happened that day with Mohamed Moulud frightened him very much because of how the soldiers might react, and so he rushed off to say to his wife Nisha, "Woman, woman, get all our belongings ready because we are moving this very night. Your son has burned the Spanish flag, and they will surely come and get us all."

My grandmother didn't think much of it either and answered, "Let them come, what's going to happen? The person who did all of this is just a child."

But Omar was adamant that they leave the area. He communicated his decision to his closest neighbors—our family friends, *Ahel* Mohamed Lechereyef—and that very night they all took down their *jaimas*, packed up their belongings, and loaded everything onto their camels. They rode all night, putting several kilometers between themselves and the place where they thought the soldiers might go looking for them.

At dawn, the area was hit by strong winds that completely wiped out their tracks and that left them all feeling a bit relieved. They reached the well at Buer Aulad Daud in the morning and discovered that it was unusable because a camel had fallen into it and contaminated the water. In spite of everything, they decided to camp there, remove the animal from the well piece by piece, clean the well, drain it, and wait for it to fill up again with clean water. The following morning, they replenished their water supply, packed up, and headed toward the area of Zug, to the south of the territory, with the strong winds continuing unabated. Finally, on the fifth day of their journey, they arrived at the mouth of the famous Zug well. They spent a day there watering their camels until some Spanish patrol officers in convertibles showed up unexpectedly. My grandfather's friend, Deid Uld Futa, was with them, and he came up to say hello to everyone. My grandfather gave him a signal when the officer who was with him asked my grandfather if he knew anything about a family that was camping in the vicinity of the road construction site. My grandfather Omar responded that they did not have any information about that region, because they had spent the summer in the Zug area. His collusion with the translator, our family friend, saved my uncle from being punished by the soldiers.

Our Paternal Great-Grandfather

Our great-grandfather on our father's side was Mohamed El Alem Uld Abdelaziz Uld Abiay, also known as Awah. His son Mohamed was a great poet and a generous person who was loved by many of his contemporaries. Mohamed Uld Awah's generosity toward his guests was the theme of some poems that Mama used to recite in conversations about the Saharawi tea ceremony and its rituals, or when she was giving her opinion on the set of utensils, known as اماعين اتاي *main atai*, that were used to prepare the tea.

She maintained that a proper tea ceremony had to meet the requirements of the Mauritanian poet and singer Sedum, alias Sedum the Great, that are immortalized in a poem that he dedicated to his host, my great-uncle Mohamed Uld Awah. Sedum simply calls him Mohamed Lawah in this poem, abbreviating his surnames to achieve rhythm and symmetry.

التاي اللا هو مولاه	محمد لواه التنزاه
تعدال اتا يو ماهو حوص	مخلا محمد لواه
ويجي طايب ماهو محيوص	عند الكيمة يوطلع ماه
يعرف كد اليسكي من رؤص	والسخار اللي يتولاه
من ماه من احسن تملوص	الناس للي تشرب وياه
من الطوص الماهو مخصوص	برادو معدن واسبناه
كسانو بالنص المنصوص	واللا ما فتنا وصفناه

79

Jubilant Mohamed Lawah,

tea meister.

Soon his water boils,

the tea is served leisurely,

and the person who makes it knows

how many to serve and to please,

and does not pause to count

those who are going to have some.

His teapot of noble mineral,

his indescribable gleaming porcelain tray,

are beyond compare.

And what are these made of?

Porcelain cups, glass,

and as for the colors,

there are red and green ones,

light, dark, and soft shades.

He describes the superior quality of our great-uncle's tea set in the ballad, which from my recollection, our paternal grandmother, Ghalia Mint Yusuf Uld El Atik, also used to reminisce about. I believe the story might be set at the end of the nineteenth century, when ceramic, porcelain, and colored glasses were valued utensils that were not accessible to just anybody and were perhaps a status symbol at a time of real progress among the nomads of the Sahara.

Mama recounted that Awah was much sought after as a host and that the *ghazi* would often get together with him and other nomads for a good time as they went on their long expeditions throughout the territory, defending the borders of the Sahara from foreign intruders. The hospitality and kindness that Mohamed Uld Awah showed in his day can be inferred from this next poem, whose authorship is unknown to my family:

محمد لواه التنزاه	اتاي اللا هو مولاه
امن الكيمى يطلع ماه	و يجي طايب ماهو محيوس
و الساخر اللي يتولاه	يعرف كد اللي يسكي من روس
اللي تشرب وياه	
محمد لواه التنزاه	مارينا نظر من نظراه
بيه اللي مولانا غلاه	مولى هول و مولى شهوات
حيوان فايت فالفوات	و لا يكبل يستدبر
و ذاك الخاطر من عز	في اقلوب الغيدات
الي رات ينشك اعليها لگدر	عن شي متمكرظ متكبر
بيه اللي مولانا واساه	محمد لواه التنزاه
الناس اللي تشرب وياه	هذا ماه عن حسبتها منقوص
براد معدن واسبناه	امن الطوس الماه موصوف
امعينو طوس الا تنزاه	مطروحين فطبلة تبهر

81

هذا و السكر يسو كد   اغلاه اتم الا يكسر

و اذبيحة لغنم ماتخطاه   و لا يخطاه اشهر ما ينحر

وكتن فات اللي فات   من شكر باقي شكر اوخر

Mohamed Lawah, opulence incarnate,
host of the tea ceremony.
From the very beginning
his teapot starts to bubble over with water,
and he carefully serves it hot.
His *sajar* knows how many guests he is going to treat.

Mohamed Lawah, opulence incarnate,
is incomparable among his compatriots,
because God made him unique on his altar.
Lord of the arts,
lord of festivities,
lord of the capriciousness
devoted to pleasure,
lord who eschews austerity,
lord in whose dwelling
and on the altar of whose *jaima*
reigns Cupid.

A Gentleman,
he is elegant and beyond trivialities,
because God made him Mohamed Lawah, opulence
    incarnate,

peerless distinguished host of the tea ceremony.
Those who taste his tea
do not wane in their appreciation.
His tea set is made of good metal,
soft cloths embroidered with pheasant feathers.
Magnificent tea utensils,
Napkins, embroidered with pheasant feathers,
displayed on a shining embossed tray,
made of untarnished copper.

The Awah Family

Detu remembered more stories about our paternal family than my own father. I once asked her about that famous saying among Saharawis, "Waiting for Uld Awah's rice," although I somewhat remembered having heard about it from my grandparents Hamadi and Ghalia when I was little. I often heard many people distorting the story and its origin, and so I said to Detu, "Mama, I am tired of hearing people misrepresenting this story. It has ended up becoming a joke when, in reality, it is a literary device that even our poets use to denote an improbable event. Tell me what you really know about it, since you knew Dad's parents and lived with them for a long time."

Detu answered my question, saying, "No story, not even the Holy Qur'an, the Bible, or the Torah, has ever survived without distortions and changes to its original form; of course, there have always been revisionists in religious and social matters. The events that have had the most impact on people have undergone several interpretations throughout every culture and period. The same goes for our oral histories, which change in one way or another with each new generation. However, as to this story, its original version is still alive and intact, especially among the inhabitants of Tiris, where Mohamed El Alem, alias Awah, lived."

My mother went on explain the story to me, which she knew quite well: "I learned this story when I was a little girl from my father Omar, before I met the *Ahel* Awah family. But later on, I heard it from the lips of your grandparents, who told me the very same version. The children of Mohamed Uld El Jalil, the legendary warrior and scholar, who was a great friend of Mohamed El Alem Awah's, also told me the story exactly the way it happened."

Awah was a very generous man, and he was also known to be a great orator. He had many friends among the nomads of Tiris, and he was very funny, a trait that was peculiar to the inhabitants of that land. Legend has it that he once hosted some friends who were passing through in a caravan and who coincidentally camped that night in his welcoming *jaima* in Tiris. He set up a separate *jaima* for the guests, away from the family's *jaimas*, so that they would be more comfortable and could sleep whenever they wanted without disturbing the children in the family. Those were times when food was scarce—they were particularly tough years for the nomads—and the inhabitants of Tiris basically lived on camel meat and milk. They were short on grains, and only a lucky few could treat their guests to rice.

Awah offered his friends some tea, as was customary among Saharawis whenever they had guests. Later, he served them the roasted meat of a fine lamb that he had slaughtered for them that night. The roast would always be followed by rice, but Awah did not have any on that occasion. According to Mama, when the guests finished eating the meat, another round of tea was prepared, and they continued chatting pleasantly until very late. One of them then inquired if there was going to be anything else, to which Awah responded, "Yes, yes, there is some rice, but we must wait, it is being prepared."

He then left the guests' *jaima* as if he were going to inquire about how soon the rice would be ready. Actually, he just went back to his own *jaima*. Awah wanted to play a good prank on his friends. He wanted people to talk about it the next day and everyone to get a good laugh from that story for a long time. And so, he settled in his *jaima* to go to bed, but before that he asked his wife how his friends were doing, and she answered, "*Elgoum* are waiting for our rice. We will really have a good laugh tomorrow."

The guests spent the whole night waiting for Awah's nonexistent rice until, one by one, they were overcome by sleep. And to this very day, this story is often talked about among Saharawis as an anecdote whose true origins remain unclear to most people.

Beloved Tiris, Land of Our Ancestors

Mama, too, loved hearing the stories that were told by her brother Moulud, my prodigious uncle who was very much adored in the family because of his mischievousness and the practical jokes that he played on his friends and other people. He had learned how to read and write, together with my mother, when he was very little. She used to say that he was the smartest one in the family, a good hunter, an expert camel trainer, and an excellent *deyar*. During one of my trips to the Saharawi refugee camps, after my mother had passed away, I asked Moulud to tell me something that he remembered about Detu, something that she would have loved to hear or recount herself. My uncle responded without having to ponder it too much: "Your mother was the joy of our family, she deeply loved Tiris, that beautiful land that we are all fighting for, and I think the best way to have her with us is to evoke the poems that the scholar Chej Luali and the other legendary sages composed about Tiris. She memorized and recited those poems when she was young because she adored that beautiful place and its warm people, particularly the scholars who knew and sang about Tiris."

Moulud explained to me that Mama would always recite a certain poem by one of the Tiris scholars whenever her homeland was mentioned at a social gathering. The poem is in praise of Tiris, and it shows how much its nomadic inhabitants loved that land. Detu was not fanatical in her love for her land; rather, she was simply honest in expressing her feelings about her birthplace.

Her love for Tiris reminds me of the story of Michel de Vieuchange, a romantic French adventurer who in 1930 embarked on a daring voyage, obsessed by the desire to see the old fort in Smara—the only city in Western Sahara founded by a Saharawi, the anti-colonial theologian and scholar Chej Malainin. Vieuchange was a fragile young man. However, he had the worthy ambition of making that mysterious city that he loved, and that he wanted to show to the whole world, go down in history.

The fort and its mosque in the middle of an immense desert made an impression on Vieuchange after his harrowing journey. He left a message in which he explained what a spectacular vision it was, and which also summed up what the city meant to him, in words that made him sound like a romantic hero: "See Smara and die."

Before leaving the city, in which he had spent barely three hours, the young man recorded the adventure that cost him his life in a message inside a glass bottle. The message was discovered years later by Spanish troops who entered the Saharawis' holy city. Vieuchange's odyssey, which is documented in a book that was published posthumously, now forms part of the History, with a capital "H," of the Sahara, as various writers and scholars have noted. The story was also documented by the anthropologist Julio Caro Baroja in his magnificent treatise on Saharawi society, *Estudios saharianos*,[9] which was published in 1955.

Detu's love for Tiris, her land, was similar, except she was born there and enjoyed living there in her childhood and in her youth. My mother had a saying akin to "See Smara and die." She used to say something very similar about Tiris: "I wouldn't want to be that person who never saw Tiris all covered in green." Sometimes I would say to her in jest, "Mama, I have an advantage, you know, because I have seen Tiris at war, at peace, during droughts, all green, but always very pretty." She would respond, "You were raised on the rich milk of her camels, which tastes like *asckaf*."

---

9. *Saharawi Studies.*

Of course, she, too, experienced the land in all those situations. There was, for example, the war that took place between 1957 and 1958. Those years are known among Saharawis as *Am Elhuyum*, which refers to the time when Spain and France joined forces to change their colonial borders, to the detriment of the Saharawis.

This is the poem that my mother really enjoyed reciting in her conversations about Tiris:

كَانْ آنَزلْتُ اللّي غيرها   تِيرس مَا تكُبِّلَ لخلاَط

نَظمْ آخْليِل اَعْلَى دَيْرها   راني خليت آنتَــاجّاط

There is no mistaking Tiris,
even when one is camped
outside her borders.
My song to her beauty in Jlil[iv]
remains in Ntayat.

Ntayat is a mountain in southern Tiris, situated southeast of the town of Tichla. This poem is about Ntayat, the Tirisian hill where Chej Mohamed El Mami—the illustrious Saharawi poet and scholar who is mentioned indirectly through his great work "Jlil"—is buried. Chej Mohamed El Mami is buried in the valley of Ntayat hill

---

iv. A work of poetry by the wise and erudite Tirisian Chej Mohamed El Mami.

افي منحر in *menhru*, as we say in Hassaniya, which means the south-facing slope of a mountain. The older generations who are passing on, the ones who cannot return to their beloved Tiris to rest forever in eternity, as my mother had always wished, have been robbed of Chej Mohamed El Mami's good fortune.

Nana and Lehbeila

I remember when my older sister Nana left to go and live in Villa Cisneros, known today as Dajla. My mother wanted our little sister Lehbeila, who was the youngest at the time and the one of whom I was most fond, to go with her. While we were preparing for their journey and the presents were being packed into some dark blue metal trunks, I heard my aunts saying that my older sister was going to take the child with her. I loved all my sisters equally but, at the time, my little sister was the center of attention in the whole family, and it was very difficult for me to part with her.

My father had to agree to it. Although he adored the little one, it was Nana's first time leaving home, and he wanted the little girl to keep her company while she, Nana, got used to and adapted to the city and to her new situation. I still remember the song that my father used to sing to Lehbeila to lull her to sleep when she was a year old. When my sister was little, her navel stuck out a bit because of a hernia, and my father used that in the song that went something like this: "Whoever does not have an outie has been had, he doesn't have a shirt, he doesn't have a sweater." The rhyme in Hassaniya is quite funny, and it would make my mother laugh because my father didn't know how to compose poetry, but according to her that lullaby turned out pretty well for him.

The day when my sister was supposed to travel, I got hold of my little sister Lehbeila while my mother was busy with the packing and said to her, "You're coming with me. I'm going to buy you some candy, and then I'll take you to a *talha* to play on the swing."

That *talha* was a hundred-year-old tree with an enormous perpetually verdant crown that was always full of birds, and it was the children's favorite gathering spot for games. I believed that if I hid my sister, I would be able to prevent them from taking her away, but my parents had already made their decision. I thought that if we kept playing in the tree, which was far from the town, they would forget to take her with them. However, finally they found us and took us back home. In the end, my little sister left with her older sister.

Mama was very sensitive, and sometimes she, too, would break down, as would any mother facing certain situations and decisions, such as being separated from two of her daughters, as was the case this time. That day we all said goodbye to my sisters, the oldest one and the youngest, and that night my house felt worse than a desert to me.

I went into the kitchen to get the tea utensils ready for my father, who had just come back from work, and I saw that my mother, who was alone in the kitchen, had tears in her eyes. When she realized I was there, she tried to hide her tears. I picked up the tray and went into the living room, where my father and a neighbor were chatting. I placed the utensils in front of my father, and then I left the house for a bit. Later, I came home, and when we were all sitting in the living room, my father's friend said to my mother in a familiar and friendly tone, "Well, well, well, Jadiyetu is weeping, but all women get married and make their own lives far away from their families."

She responded that the house felt empty and burst into tears. When I saw that, I bolted out of the house and went to weep outside. Later, I went to my grandmother's to calm down for a while by talking to my aunts.

My mother was a very strong woman. However, like any other mother, she, too, would buckle sometimes under the strange and unexpected situations that life and its inexorable journey brought her way.

IV.

MAMA'S DECISION AND THE
1975 EXODUS: EXILE

*Death does not take away our loved ones. On the
contrary, it keeps them for us.*
                              —François Mauriac

My family was living in the town of Auserd, and I was
fifteen years old that November in 1975. I believe it was
the end of the month, because I remember us hearing the
news about the Green March and Franco's dying moments on the Voice of Free Sahara radio station.

All these events took place between the months of October and December in 1975. We were still in Auserd,
which, at the time, was under the control of the Polisario
Front after Spain's unexpected withdrawal.

The metropolis, Spain, had abandoned us under the
treacherous agreement that it had signed with Morocco
and Mauritania on November 14, 1975. Thus was the territory divided up and occupied by the two regimes, Morocco's and that of Mauritania's Ould Daddah.

Our World Falls Apart

On December 10, 1975, La Güera, which was then known as Cabo Blanco, managed to resist the siege by Mauritanian troops, who were involved in the war because of the terms of the illegal Tripartite Madrid Accord[v] signed by Spain, Morocco, and Mauritania. Faced with the imminent danger of the Mauritanian or Moroccan army bringing the conflict with them into Auserd, the Polisario decided to evacuate the civilian population from the city to prevent the civilians from being used as human shields. There were two large camps on the outskirts of the city, one in the West and another in the North, some thirty kilometers away.

Our family moved to the Shig camp, situated in northern Auserd, where it was possible to find good water in the *ishiguin*. A temporary camp had been set up there, and people were saying that we would only be there for a few days, that Algeria would intervene to protect us from the invading armies, and that we would be going back home again soon. Those were some of the rumors that were circulating among the people at the camp.

I recall that at night, Mama would ask us to get the radio so we could listen to the news. My older sister and I

---

v. This agreement, signed by three dictatorial governments, was never published in the *Boletín Oficial del Estado* (*Official Gazette of Spain*), and, therefore, it has no legal standing.

would tune in to Voice of Free Sahara on the Philips radio that we had at home.

Mama understood the gravity of the situation, and she attentively followed the news about the fighting that was going on in Auserd between the Saharawi army and the army of the invader, Moktar Ould Daddah. My father and my uncles joined the militias who were responsible for protecting and running the camp, and my older sister helped at a small dispensary, a white tent with the Dutch Red Cross insignia on it. People stocked up on the aid that was coming in from the city, and some families brought the little that was left in their small shops after the withdrawal of the Spanish administration.

Spain abandoned the town, leaving nothing in working order. The power station that supplied energy ground to a halt, and the diesel barrels that fed the only generator that remained in the town became riddled with holes.

The schools shuttered their classrooms. The playgrounds were strewn with books, and the doors were all ajar. "Civilization" turned its back on everything that had been achieved over more than a hundred years in Auserd and the rest of the Sahara. The only hospital in the city was evacuated and was left without even the most basic first-aid equipment.

Bullenna Uld Nawa, a Saharawi assistant who worked with the Spanish administration at the hospital, took it upon himself to secure and manage the few drugs that he could salvage to treat the most urgent cases, especially those that involved children and pregnant women. The bakeries in the city also closed their doors, and the familiar aroma of warm bread faded—that bread known as "the ration of such and such a family" that we would pick up from the colonial government provisions store after school every day at noon. The inhabitants had a very slim chance of survival in the midst of a situation that was neither nomadic nor sedentary. It was simply a case of abandonment, in its most cruel and shameful form, and it was mostly the defenseless civilians who were left to pay the price.

My former brother-in-law, Enna Mohamed Fadel, recalls that he and the other young men who were working at the time at Miferma, the French company that was mining iron in Zouérat, Mauritania, decided to enlist in the Polisario forces through their office in Nouadhibou. From there, they went on to the Saharawi city of Cabo Blanco, La Güera, which was taken over by Saharawi fighters after Spain's departure. Cabo Blanco was only some three kilometers away from the Mauritanian city.

Once they got to Cabo Blanco, they began training to defend it, and on December 10, 1975, they were attacked by Mauritania in fulfillment of the terms of the Tripartite Madrid Accord that had left the territory under Moroccan and Mauritanian occupation. For twelve days, they held out against the Mauritanian army, until they received the order on December 22 to retreat to a town called Safya. But by January 8, 1976, the Polisario had already evacuated the residents of Auserd, where there was fierce fighting going on, to the valleys of Shig and Amzeili.

I recall one afternoon when we suddenly found that the camps where we were taking refuge had been completely surrounded by military vehicles in tactical positions with guns trained on every *jaima* at the camp.

People were coming out of their *jaimas*, confused, to find out what was going on. Some people were holding up Saharawi flags as a sign of welcome, and the women were greeting them with *zgarit*. They thought that the soldiers were Polisario or Algerian soldiers who were bringing us aid, which was the rumor that was going around in those days. However, we quickly realized that we had fallen into the hands of the enemy.

The troops had assumed combat positions all around the camp, and we could clearly see some Black soldiers, which was reassuring to some people who said that because they were Mauritanians, we could at least resolve matters with them in Hassaniya. Others said with some relief, "It's a good thing they are not *shluha*," meaning that they were not Moroccans.

The soldiers entered the *jaimas*, searching for young men and Saharawi fighters, who would sometimes pass through the camps to be treated for their wounds. At first, I hid behind some trunks, but when I realized that it might look suspicious if they found me, I came out before the soldiers arrived to search our *jaima*. They led me to the place where they were assembling the men at the camp.

The soldiers rounded up all the men and the young boys to take us back to our town, which they had already taken over. Among them were my father, my uncles, and many acquaintances. I still remember that as they were taking me toward the cars, I passed by some men who were lying face down with their hands tied and with soldiers pointing guns at their heads, while other prisoners were climbing into the vehicles. I immediately recognized my two uncles, Mohamed and Mohamed Moulud, among them. The Mauritanians wanted to use all the people in the town as human shields. I also remember the case of Hamudi Uld Ahmed Baba, an important member of the first advisory council, which had just returned from meeting with the Algerian president, Houari Boumédiène, following the dissolution of the first *Yemaa*. Hamudi had just traveled back to the camps to join his wife, who was about to give birth, and his children. He was captured by the soldiers and tortured, which left him with permanent damage to his back.

Later, after the soldiers had left, my mother, a friend of hers called El Bagra Mint El Kenti, and my sister Nana gathered all my books and our family's Spanish documents, including our social security cards, our family record book, my parents' and my older sister's identification documents, and our photographs. They put everything in a plastic bag and buried it under the southern side of a large rock in the middle of the plains. Mama was afraid of suffering reprisals at the hands of the Mauritanians and the Moroccans, who saw people carrying Spanish identification documents as unbelievers and as people who rejected the occupiers.

My aunt Alia, however, refused to get rid of her documents, and when our family was moved back to Auserd, they exchanged them for a *Carte d'identité mauritanie*[10] that had the number of the Spanish identification document on the back of it. A friend of mine, who was hired by the Mauritanian administration to carry out this mandatory change of identity documents for all Saharawis living under Mauritanian occupation at the time, told me about the arrangement. My friend explained to me that the

---

10. A Mauritanian identity card.

young Saharawi workers themselves had come up with the idea of preserving the Spanish identification numbers as a means of leaving some record of that compulsory change of identity.

That is just one example of the ghastly operation undertaken by Mauritania to erase any traces of our Saharawi identity and to destroy our historical ties to Spain. The loss of our Spanish papers meant that my father could never assert his right to draw a pension for the twenty-five years that he had served as a Spanish soldier with the Nomad Troops.

People were wondering what they were planning to do with us, unaware of the fate of the men who had been taken back to town, including my father and my uncles Moulud and Mohamed. The military commanders addressed the residents and told us that they would return the following day to take us back to the town. People were frightened, realizing that they would be used as human shields against the attacks and fighting going on in the area.

Aunt Alia saved me that afternoon from being taken away by the soldiers. She begged the head of the unit to let me go, lying to him that I was mentally ill. That same afternoon, when they left with all the men from the camp, my mother and my sister, fearing that the soldiers might take me away, told me to go to a Polisario base in

Gleybat Legleya, where they would know how to protect me. One of my mother's brothers, Boiba, had joined the ranks of the Polisario in 1974 after deserting from a Spanish military patrol unit in which he was serving as a soldier with the Nomad Troops. Perhaps she drew strength from her belief that I would be safe if I joined him.

That moment was the beginning of my true exodus as a fifteen-year-old child in the midst of an avalanche of families who were fleeing from the war and from the people descending upon us from the north; they terrified us. They were bad news, and the impression that we had of them always revolved around the Saharawi saying that our grandparents would repeat to us in reference to Morocco: *Etal Beit Shar*, meaning "The North is a house of enmity" or "Wickedness reigns at the northern borders." And so it was that, when I fled, I joined the thousands of people who were leaving behind their homes and their land.

My Triangular Exile

Maktuba preordained my life to be defined by a triangular exile. First of all, I spent three years at a boarding school in Algeria for the children of the fallen in the Algerian war of independence against the French colonizers. I still remember that boarding school, قدماء المجاهدين العربي بن امهيدي مركز بنين و بنات, the El Arbi Ben Mheidi Center for the Sons

101

and Daughters of the Fallen, in the city of Mecheria, in the *wilaya* of Saida.

We were among a group of Saharawi students who had arrived from different parts of the Saharawi territory during the exodus, and we finished high school there. We were taught entirely in Spanish by Saharawi teachers, young university students who had not yet graduated when Spain abandoned the territory. Berrura, Dahay, Bulahi, Chej, Bachir, Nino, and Mohamed are all a part of our history, and I will remember them forever with deep appreciation.

My second destination was Cuba, another very important land in our long journey as exiles from place to place, where I completed my studies in telecommunications. Finally, after a very long time in the camps, I settled in Spain—the former colonial center—where I would have to go through three universities in search of another degree that would enable me to work and help Mama. She had ended up penniless, together with the rest of my family, in the refugee camps after the signing of the peace plan. However, it would be many more years before I would arrive at the third stage of my exile. My mother would have no idea of my whereabouts from the night when she said goodbye to me, so long ago at the Shig camp in Auserd, until the summer of 1984, a decade after the war began. I had returned to the refugee camps in Tindouf from Cuba for some nineteen days to spend time with her and to prove to her that I was still alive. For ten years, she had not seen me, and she therefore believed that I had died during the early years of my flight.

That holiday came as a real surprise to me after a meeting with the then Saharawi minister of education, Mohamed Lamin Uld Ahmed, who was also one of the memorable founders of the Polisario Front. He had come to visit us on the island and to bring us news of the progress that was being made in the struggle against Morocco. At the end of his talk, the minister read out my name from a sheet of paper and said, "Bahia Mahmud, please remain in the room."

It turned out that the Saharawi leader had been my mother's neighbor at the same camp in Hagunia and he knew her very well. When she found out that he was the minister of education, she went over to his *jaima* with a request that, if it was true that I was alive and that I was studying in a foreign land, she would like to see me after so many years of being uncertain as to my whereabouts. And as a result of all of that, I ended up on this surprise journey without a passport and traveling on a laissez-passer issued by the Algerian embassy in Havana. I had lost my papers not long after I had arrived in Cuba. That laissez-passer enabled me to finally travel back to my family, although it did create some problems for me when I arrived at the Barajas Airport. An elderly policeman looked at it at length and finally said to me, "You, stay here until the passengers leave."

A while later he called me and, without looking at the document, said, "This document is written in French, and it's of no use, I can't make anything of it." "Don't worry," I explained, "this document is a laissez-passer that is valid even in China, whether it's written in French, English, or any other language, and it was issued to me by the Algerian embassy in Cuba because I lost my passport."

The two of us became embroiled in a fierce argument, until finally I said to him, "I'm not Algerian, I'm a Saharawi student, I would like to speak to your supervisor, and I demand to see the manager of Air Algérie for this airport." A few minutes later, another policeman said to me, "Take it easy, we're going to figure this out."

He picked up the phone and called another officer, who showed up right away. I explained everything to him and complained about how I had been treated and about the ignorance of the officer who had rudely told me that my document was useless.

The Air Algérie official arrived, listened to the two Spanish policemen's explanations, and then spoke to me after greeting me warmly, thinking that I was Algerian. I told him that I was a Saharawi student who had arrived from the Caribbean with a laissez-passer issued by the Algerian embassy and that the policeman had told me that it was of no use because it was written in French. A fierce argument ensued between the officer and the representative of the Algerian airline. There were five other students traveling with me, two boys and three girls, who had been waiting for me from the beginning and who had gone to alert the Algerian official when they saw that things were getting complicated. My friends could no longer wait for me because a bus had arrived to take them to the hotel. They were supposed to stay there for two days in transit before traveling on to Algiers, because there were no seats on the flight that was leaving that day. Finally, the Algerian representative took me out of the passport control area to a cafeteria. I told him that I didn't have a cent on me and that we only had a few dollars between us for the journey, in case we wanted to have some coffee or call the Saharawi embassy to be picked up once we arrived in Algiers.

The same afternoon, I boarded a plane bound for Algiers, without my friends, because I could neither leave the airport nor stay there for much longer. When I arrived at the airport, there was no one to meet me there either, because they weren't expecting any of us to arrive the same day. After waiting for several hours, I got a taxi and asked to be taken to the Saharawi diplomatic mission on calle Franklin Roosevelt. The taxi driver knew where it was, as he had regularly driven other Saharawis there. When we arrived, he parked in front of the building, which was guarded by policemen, and I said to him, "Wait for me because I don't have any money on me."

I noticed that he looked puzzled when I said I didn't have any money. I told a Saharawi official who attended to me about my situation. He paid the taxi driver and took me to the cafeteria, because I told him that I hadn't eaten in almost two days. I had been separated from my family for ten years, and I had become a child of the war. My family thought I was missing, and they had had no news of me in all that time, save for the letters that I would send to my older sister, but my mother was never convinced by what my sister would tell her.

My Family's Exodus and Mama's Illness

My family settled in the Tindouf refugee camps after the peace agreement that was signed between Mauritania and the Saharawi government in 1979. When the war with Mauritania ended, all the inhabitants who had been living under the Mauritanian occupation were handed over to the Saharawi authorities, and they went to live in the refugee camps because Morocco had occupied the territory that Mauritania relinquished when it withdrew.

But in 1975, the war in the Sahara had reached its peak, and Auserd, where my whole family was based, fell under Mauritanian military occupation for four years. Mama fell ill during the period of the occupation, and through the contacts of her great friend Beisat Uld Deih Uld Boyda, she was able to get the Mauritanian authorities to airlift her in a small plane to the Mauritanian capital, Nouakchott, for treatment.

Both my older sister Aichanana and Beisat accompanied her on that journey. That was the first time she showed symptoms of hepatitis, the result of the food deprivation and lack of vitamins and proteins that afflicted the Saharawi population after Spain abandoned the territory and its inhabitants.

Mama was hospitalized in the Mauritanian capital until she got better. Later, she was transferred to the home of my paternal uncle Mohamed Uld Awah, an important Saharawi businessman in Mauritania, where he had settled from a very early age. After a few months, she was feeling better, had sufficiently recovered, and was much stronger, so she decided to return to the Sahara. My sister, however, had another problem that my mother was aware of and hoped could be resolved.

My older sister had gotten married in November 1975, the very month that the territory was invaded by Morocco and Mauritania. Barely one week after their wedding, her husband joined the ranks of the first Polisario guerillas. He was wounded and captured by the Mauritanian army at a time when it was one of the invaders and a signatory to the previously mentioned Tripartite Madrid Accord between Spain, Morocco, and Mauritania, the cause of our misfortune. Months later, my sister found out that her husband was being held in a military prison very close to Nouakchott.

Aichanana was looking for an influential person in the Saharawi community who could help her gain access to the prison where her husband was being held so she could visit him while she was with my mother in the capital. At that time, the family's situation was quite dire and was a constant torment for my mother, with all our misfortunes piling onto the illness from which she was recuperating. She presumed that I had gone missing during the exodus, my siblings were alone with my father, they were all little, and the family's financial situation was getting more and more difficult. My father and my uncles Moulud and Lajdar struggled very hard to feed and care for our large extended family.

Mama's Kindness

All her life, Mama supported the weak and those who were most in need, but even more so during the years that she lived in the camps, those very tough years when there were times of extreme poverty. According to my sisters, when Detu found out that there was a pregnant woman in their neighborhood, she would tell all her daughters, "You must help her. When you get a little bit of meat, take her some, because it's a human duty, and God will reward you one day."

It is customary among Saharawis that when a woman becomes pregnant, her husband provides her with meat for all her meals. Right from the beginning of their pregnancy, Saharawi women crave meat, and people say that their bodies require it for the development of the fetus. However, during the first years of refugeehood and scarcity, many men did not have the means to fulfill that family obligation, and hence Mama's concern for the pregnant women. She would say to us, "We must help a pregnant woman in this way. God and his prophet advise us to take care of pregnant women."

Whenever my father got the opportunity to buy a kilo of meat for the family, she would take it, divide it up, and distribute it in the neighborhood as she saw fit, always among the neediest women, the pregnant ones, or the elderly women who lived alone.

Because of my mother's kindness and guilelessness, we played pranks on her on numerous occasions, and we particularly enjoyed hiding our identity from her by disguising ourselves. We would pretend to be members of a neighboring family that was in a difficult situation and needed help. My female cousins and my sister Suadu were always the ones responsible for carrying out these endearing shenanigans.

At times we would wear a disguise, and at other times we would disguise our voices and stand outside our *jaima* to pull our prank on Mama. "Hello, Jadiyetu, I am your neighbor's son. She's feeling a bit under the weather, and she says to ask you if you have some herbal medicine to soothe her headache."

Detu would search quickly for something that could help the supposedly sick person, opening all the cupboards, and as she was searching, she would ask, looking worried and sad, "When did the pain start? Tell her to take such and such." She always had those feelings for the weak and the sick. Sometimes, when she herself was ill from an asthma attack and could barely move, she would try to get up and do a good deed for someone who needed her. She was incapable of not being helpful to others. Mahatma Gandhi alluded to people of that nature who were concerned about the well-being of others regardless of how difficult their own lives were: "No one can do good in one area of his or her life while doing harm in another. Life is an indivisible whole."

My grandmother Nisha mentioned that, as a child, Detu wanted to be a grown-up woman. To her, fifty-something was the most stable and humane age. She considered it to be ideal for helping without being judgmental and without harming anyone. The great Greek philosopher Plato alluded to that pure kindness that I found to be inherent in my mother when he said, "By seeking the well-being of our fellow humans we find our own."

Clearly, Mama found her own well-being on numerous occasions in the circumstances around her through seeking the well-being of her fellow human beings as a sisterly, sensitive, and humane woman. She devoted herself to cultivating verdant bushes that provided shade for the weary and sustenance for any guests who came into her *jaima*.

To describe Detu's work as a mother, a teacher, and a caring woman, we could turn to the image of Mother Teresa of Calcutta. Obvious differences aside, she was the anonymous Mother Teresa of the Sahara. I will never forget the countless times I unsuccessfully searched all over our house for my clothes because Mama had discreetly given them away to a needy person.

She would often say that when we give charity—*sadga*—to those in need, we should never do so to show that we are strong, rich, or better than they are, and we should never give it in front of other people but rather privately and in secret. That way, the recipients of our charity would feel better, and, as Detu used to say, God would reward us for it. One felt her compassion by simply talking to her. Her serenity was striking, and her sweet face, always smiling, was tender and attentive to her guests.

There are many stories about her legendary kindness. But the one that I will never forget happened on a bitterly cold winter night in 1974, when one of our neighbors, who was suffering from a terminal illness, was at death's door. My mother got up that night and stayed with the old man, who was weeping with heartrending groans of agony, until the following morning, when he passed away in the arms of my mother and a female relative of his called Skayra, who was there alone with him. Our neighbor, an old Black man who lived alone and had no one to take care of him, was well known in the town.

My Great-Uncle Bahia Uld Awah, the Poet

My paternal great-uncle, the poet Bahia Uld Awah, lived out his final years with us at the refugee camps and was also someone who received Detu's loving care. My mother and my sisters took care of him because he was alone. He never married or had any children. In 1979, my father took him in, and our family looked after him until he passed away, a very old man by then.

Mama prepared his meals and cleaned for him. She also accompanied him when he was reciting poetry, especially when there was lively conversation during our customary tea ceremony. He called Detu "amma," which means "mom." He was more than ninety years old, and she was barely fifty, so that was paradoxical. But it was also an expression of his deep appreciation for her motherly care and her friendship.

Great-Uncle Bahia Uld Awah composed countless poems that were never compiled or published because of the difficult refugee situation and his own circumstances. But notwithstanding that, my mother and my sister Suadu memorized most of his work, which was completely oral, as is typical of the majority of the great Saharawi poets and scholars. Detu in particular memorized everything that she learned from him—mostly compositions about the struggles of the Saharawi people, memories of the land and of friends from a long time ago in his youth, and heroic deeds of legendary Saharawis, such as El Luali Mustafa Sayed, the young leader of the Polisario Front. El Luali was his inspiration for this poem:

ذالخلق ألا يزان   عاد الولي اكبر اعليه

ولعاد امعاه افميزان   لهي ميزانو يرجع بيه

A seething mass of passionate people,
Luali is their leader,
if they were to be weighed on a scale,
it would tip in their favor.

Mama, the Poet

Especially in her final years, she often spoke about the long-awaited return to the Sahara at her pleasant gatherings. She loved to talk about that because it made her feel closer to the day when she could return to the home that she had left against her will. She captured that desire in some poems that I was able to retrieve from the recollections of my sister Suadu, the most entertaining one in the family. She has a treasure trove of stories about Detu stashed away in her memory. My mother wrote these poems that reflected the dream that she longed for and that kept her going during her years in exile. In exile, Mama continued the fight to ensure that the desire to return to her land did not end up being a mere fantasy.

My sister told me that my mother composed this poem in 1985, when the war was at its peak. She had the feeling that our struggle would inevitably have a happy ending.

مول الملك المالو تشبيه   انا نطلب مول القدرء

لستقلال اللي نحظر فيه   يعطي يلا للهل الصحرء

To the Almighty, my cry,
Lord of all thrones, the incomparable,
grant the owners of the Sahara freedom,
so that I may enjoy it.

114

Detu had recited this poem to me years ago, but I had forgotten it. After she left us, I asked my sister Suadu if she recalled any of Mama's sayings or notable stories, which was when she surprised me with the poem.

Suadu told me that Mama used to compose short poems during the pleasant conversations that she would have over the tea ceremony with her friends. However, according to Suadu, she didn't give much importance to her poetic creations, and she also felt that we were too little at the time to memorize them, which is why almost all her poems are now lost.

Mama, Our Eternal Guide

It has been four years since her passing, and our home at the camp in the *wilaya* of El-Aaiún, "Mama's *jaima*," continues to be the place where her children and grandchildren get together, chat, eat, and sleep. After Jadiyetu left us, my youngest sister, Salca, with the help of our older sister Aichanana, moved with her children into Mama's house and made it a home for everybody.

My younger brother Alati also lived there for a while, and my partner and I stay there when we visit them from Spain. One can feel her spirit in the house, and we all reminisce about her through her anecdotes and stories when we get together with friends and family who come to visit us.

During one of my recent trips to the camps, Salca said to me one day, "Do you know that I hosted a famous group of Hassaniya poets here? And they left me a poem written in honor of our family and as a tribute to Mama." Immediately, I said to her, "Look for it and let me record it so that it doesn't get lost."

Salca, or Salquita, as I call her, could not recall which of the guests had written the poem. She brought me a sheet cut out from one of those notebooks with double lines, and my eyes immediately went in search of the signature. I saw that at the bottom of the text, it said, "Sidi Brahim Salama Djdud." I subsequently had the opportunity and the pleasure of meeting Sidi Brahim, together with Badi, Beibuh, and Zaim, during a conference on the Sahara that was organized by Madrid's public universities in Tifariti in the Saharawi liberated territories. At the time, I was working with the Universidad Autónoma de Madrid at the conference, which took place from February 24 to 26, 2008. When I got a chance to step away from the discussions at the conference, I met up with Professors Alberto López Bargados, Juan Carlos Gimeno, and Juan Ignacio Robles and arranged with the latter two to have a conversation with the poets for our research project on Saharawi historical memory. I got the opportunity to meet the author of the poem, Sidi Brahim, through Badi, who is an old friend of my parents'. Sidi Brahim explained to me, "We stayed at your mother's house, and I have to tell you that you have very hospitable sisters. They hosted us for three days, during which we did not want for care or attention. This is why I wrote a poem on behalf of all of us, which we dedicated to the *Ahel* Awah and *Ahel* Embarek Fal families.

The latter is my mother's family, with whom we have been very close since time immemorial, especially with our aunts and uncles and our *Ahel* Omar grandparents. The poem seemed like a well-deserved posthumous tribute to my mother because none of these lines about our history and its protagonists would have been possible without her.

يا الشعار خير استقبال	هذا لستقبال الجيناه
واللي خلاو اهل امبارك فال	عند اللي خلاو اهل اواه
في الضهر الحاضر واللي فات	اخيام الصحرء لكبرات
اجيال التلوها لجيال	كرمت رجال و اعلايات
حميد فيهم مايوصال	اخلاق و عدات و ميزات
و حصرت عند اهل اواه الگبال	في اهل امبارك فال اتكنات
و افتفسكي في احسن لحوال	في الصيف و لخريف و شتات

I say to you, oh poets,
that warm was the welcome
that we received from our hosts,
Ahel Awah and the children of *Ahel* Embarek Fal.

Well-known families of the Sahara,

prestigious families,

generous men and women.

Today, and since time immemorial,

generation after generation of virtue,

values, traditions, and honorable behavior,

are all preserved in *Ahel* Embarek Fal.

And this quality

is an *Ahel* Awah legacy,

in the summer,

in the fall, in all of winter.

And the best thing in spring,

is this warm and splendid welcome.

When I went to their *jaima* with the research team from the university and introduced myself as Bahia Uld Awah, Skayra Mint Mohamed Elhafed, the wife of the famous Hamudi Uld Ahmed Baba, asked me, "Are you the child that I watched growing up holding on to Jadiyetu's *tarf melhfa*?"

When I confirmed her suspicions, Ahmed Baba, smiling, looked at me closely and, surprised by the way I looked with my long hair and month-old beard, said to me, "You are Jueidiyetu's son! *Ya marhba, ya marhba.* Where is Jueidiyetu?"

But when I tried to answer, I felt for a millisecond that my voice was cracking. I responded that she had left us forever on October 20, 2006. Hamudi Ahmed Baba and his wife exclaimed in unison with profound sorrow, "*Alah yarhamha.*" Skayra lifted the veil of her *melhfa* to cover her face as a sign of her sadness at the news that she had just heard and went on to ask me about my sisters, because in the 1970s only a wall separated her house and ours. She's the only one of my mother's friends from our time in Auserd who I have met since Mama passed away.

During the two hours that we spent with those family friends carrying out ethnographic research, their testimonies kept bringing back memories of our houses, one attached to the other. We used to invite each other over, and my sisters played with the only daughter in their family. I remember her name was Shaia. She was my sister Suadu's age, and she was one of the prettiest girls in the town. I remembered how my mother had told us that during the exodus, the invading soldiers captured Hamudi Uld Ahmed Baba one afternoon and tortured him in front of his wife, who had just had a baby. They took him away, with his hands tied, in their French jeep, together with my father and my uncles, that afternoon in January 1976 in the Shig valley.

That morning that I spent in the company of the *Ahel* Hamudi Uld Ahmed Baba family and Skayra, I tried to focus on our work without letting my memories take me back to my childhood after hearing Hamudi exclaim, "You are the son of Jueidiyetu!," as he affectionately called my mother in their youth. However, I felt lucky to have met those very dear friends of hers, and I remembered the advice that my mother never tired of giving us her whole life: "Whenever possible, do visit those who were our friends and our brotherly and sisterly neighbors." I think Jadiyetu's advice is closely related to Martin Luther King's words: "We have learned to fly the air like birds and swim the sea like fish, but we have not learned the simple art of living together as brothers."

Here ends the story of a great mother and a great teacher. Let it be judged by all who read this book. Each person—grandparent, parent, or child—will find in these pages that inexhaustible love of a mother and appreciate that love and its sacrifices. In so doing, we can say that we are giving back to our own mothers that which is priceless—their affection, their dedication, their sacrifice.

Epilogue

La maestra que me enseñó en una tabla de madera (*The Woman Who Taught Me on a Wooden Slate*), first published in 2011 in Spain by Sepha, now reappears in another setting for an anglophone readership thanks to the Ghanaian Canadian professor and researcher Dorothy Odartey-Wellington. She also translated and published excerpts from the book in *The Savannah Review* under the editorship of Professor Abiola Irele of Kwara State University, Nigeria, who passed away in July of 2017.

If there is anything that defines my mother, it is her personality as a humanist and her relationship with poetry. She memorized a prodigious number of poems that she would recite whenever the occasion arose, and she also composed a number of her own during her years in exile. My older sister told me that before Mama embarked on the exodus in the 1970s, she had already composed some lyrics of *tebraa*. However, she composed the majority of her poems, whose subject matter reflected her political awakening, during her years in exile in the Saharawi refugee camps. Those poems focused on her desire to leave the camps and to reclaim her territory. Several years after the publication of *La maestra que me enseñó en una tabla de madera*, I began to compile some of my mother's creative work and to discover some poems that had been dedicated to her, mostly in her youth. It is my wish that these new discoveries be included in the memories of her as a scholar and a poet. Hence this new section, in which I also add some new passages about her, because she always was, and will forever be, one of my main sources of inspiration.

My mother Jadiyetu's wish, which she impressed upon us repeatedly, was that she not die in exile. When we got together during the tea ceremony at home and, as usual, the conversation turned to the topic of our exile in Algeria and the long-awaited return to Western Sahara, or when we talked about someone who had died in exile, she would exclaim, "Oh, Lord, I pray that, while your will is inescapable, you delay it in my case and that, on the day of your choosing, it be fulfilled in my Saharawi homeland!" In the end, she did not get her last wish, which was to see her land free from occupation.

Quite often, when we reminisce about our experiences in exile, we relate them to those of other people. My own experiences remind me of the Palestinian American intellectual Edward Said, who reflected on his exile in the city of New York, where "Irish, Italian, East European

Jewish and non-Jewish, African, Caribbean, Middle and Far Eastern peoples" arrived. This diverse group of peoples, according to Said, gave rise to what he called "expatriate narratives" in his work *"Reflections on Exile" and Other Essays* (xii).

But there are also reflections on exile by many other people who have been deeply affected by the strange circumstances of exile, which have gone unnoticed in one way or another. Such is the case of my mother's oeuvre from the time of her definitive exile in Algeria, which began in 1979, until her passing in 2006.

My mother Jadiyetu Omar, just like Edward Said, albeit in a different genre and context, also reflected on exile in her "expatriate poems," such as the ones that I set out here. She composed them in 2003 while camping in her *jaima* in an area of the Saharawi liberated territories. She had managed to return for the first time after many years of living in the refugee camps in Algeria. She enjoyed a summer of freedom, far away from the harrowing conditions of exile, on a hill called Gleib Eshaar, the Woolen Hill. It is a place in the Saharawi region of Zemur where she breathed in independence along with the air and greenery of the land that she had left twenty-four years earlier because of the war and the occupation.

My mother's family, like almost all Saharawi families, ended up becoming separated in the aftermath of the

Moroccan occupation of the territory in 1975. Two of her siblings, Boilili and Alati, remained trapped in the occupied region. Alati, the eldest, passed away in 1988 without ever getting to hug his brothers and sisters again. My mother's journey to the liberated territories that summer in 2003 was all the more gratifying because she traveled in the company of her sister Boilili, who had found a way to reunite with her family. Boilili left the occupied territories, traveled across Mauritania, and managed to reach the Saharawi liberated territories to see her siblings and her mother, my grandmother Nisha. They stayed there for a month, reunited after more than three decades of being apart. They spent endless nights talking, and they made up for the many years that they had not been able to see each other, hug each other, laugh, or even cry together.

They camped at Gleib Eshaar—located between Tamreiket Hill and Tabatanet Hill—along Rus Tawiniket, which are streams that flow into the Saguia El-Hamra River, the main river of Western Sahara. My mother felt happy as she basked in exercising her sovereignty over a piece of her homeland from which she had been banished. And, as she reflected on her happiness and her strength to continue fighting back together with her people, she wrote some poems. In a subsequent telephone conversation, my Aunt Boilili, who was speaking from the occu-

pied territories, shared with me these poems that were
composed by my mother but that neither my sisters nor I
had ever heard before.

منو مانك متارك	كافي يلعڭّل امن اصبر
شوراخيام اهل امبارك	تمشي من عند اڭليب اشعر

Oh, my heart,
you have suffered enough,
but do not give up.
You go about freely
between Gleib Eshaar and
the *jaimas* of *Ahel* Embarek.[i]

In the next poem, she did not want to mention the
names of her sister Boilili and the other women who accompanied them or to give any kind of clues for fear of
reprisals at the hands of the Moroccans when they returned to the occupied territories.

من منطقتنا و الهاونا	الطافلات الجاونا
بكهولتنا و اشبابنا	بيهم ياالله اتزدنا
	و الرجوع المواطنا

Young women visit us
from our western homeland,
and they gladden our souls.

God, guide our elders and our youth.

God, I pray that soon,

we may return to our homeland.

Some of the people who were present at that long-awaited reunion are no longer with us. After Detu's departure, exile took away three of her siblings too—Yeslem, the artist with the lovely voice and jovial character; Moulud the Wise, who was famous for his skill at making himself the center of attention in conversations about history and poetry but who was also a prankster and a fun-loving person; and the delicate Jueya, an excellent conversationalist and an expert in poetry and Saharawi *houl*. In October of 2010, their mother, my grandmother Nisha Mint Bujari, the indomitable woman who valiantly and ingeniously defied the adversities of the desert, left us. She passed away in her *jaima* at the Hagunia camp, near the Algerian city of Tindouf. They are all resting now in the land of refuge, on a small hill that has brought them all together once again and forever.

To strengthen her arguments in any conversation or at those gatherings that she loved so much, my mother would always turn to passages of literature.

أُمْنِيّة ظـفِرَتْ روحـي بها زَمَنا

والـيوم أحـسَبُها أضـغاثَ أحلامَ

Desires with which I have long held my soul
> together,
and which today I consider to be castles and dreams.

This is a poem in Classical Arabic. My mother would recite it after her prayers or when she was conversing about disappointments in life, heartbreaks, and other misfortunes, such as her long exile, war, and the famine that she heard about on her ever-present Philips radio. The poem is an excerpt from a longer poem by the Egyptian mystic Ibn Elfarid (1181–1235). He was considered God's poet, and he was also known as "the sultan poet of lovers." He is regarded as one of the Sufi mystics among the poets of his time.

My mother could recite the entire poem because she had heard it so many times on the Nouakchott radio broadcasts in the seventies, a time when we could receive those broadcasts in Auserd. When she obtained a copy on tape, she enjoyed playing it on the small Philips tape recorder that my father had brought from El-Aaiún in 1970. That was just a few days after the nationalist uprising by the Sahara Liberation Organization, SLO, which was founded by the journalist Sidi Mohamed Basiri against the former colonial center—Spain under Franco.

The poem begins with the following lines, which are etched into the memories of our parents and grandparents:

نشرتُ في موكبِ العشَّاقِ أعلامي

وكانَ قبلي بُلى في الحبِّ أغلامي

I waved my flags
as the lovers' procession went by,
but at the pilgrim's destination,
the wings of love
were met with misfortune.

Whenever I speak to my sister Lehbeila, who lived with our mother the longest, her encyclopedic memory surprises me. She memorized Mama's poetry and paid a lot of attention to what Mama used to say during her years in exile. She said to me, "You have no idea. I retrieved this poem by Mama from an exercise book in which I had written in pencil. The letters are almost illegible, but I've managed to make it out by deciphering it one stanza at a time." Indeed, in the summer of 2019, thirteen years after Mama's passing, my sister Lehbeila even found some of Mama's poems that she, Lehbeila, had written down on a notepad that was kept in a trunk full of books.

حد اكول ان ظالم   مفلك لعجارم ما إكد

اتنم المغرج طالع   عند لجواد الاتم

One will experience nothing
but peace
in this valley of Laayarem Hill,
because in her bosom one finds
generous people,
always intoning poems
to the sound of a boiling teapot.

According to Lehbeila, our mother felt a real need to return to her native lands, to the region of Tiris, and to her people. However, at the same time, she was realistic and therefore aware that exile has its repercussions and that our dream of going back should not blind us to the obstacles that we still have to overcome. On the occasions—during her rare trips to the liberated territories—when Jadiyetu felt that she was exercising her freedom, she would become "uncontrollably" inspired, and her poetic and erudite soul would transport her to Tiris, her land of poetry, and to the majestic hills of Auserd.

One of those occasions arose as a result of a meeting with several members of her family in the liberated area, specifically on the hill and along the streams of Laayarem.

She was inspired by the captivating nature of the hill, which reminded her of the landscape of her native region, Tiris. Thus began a poetic dialogue between her and her young cousin, Jadiyetu Mint Rahel, who, moved by the memories that the place evoked in my mother and fascinated by the crystalline white color of the pebbles on the hill where they would gather in the mornings, composed the following *gaf*:

احذ خدجتو ذى الفضيل   سبحان اللي خلق ذى الرگ

و املي كانت جميل   ازگ ذو القيدات رد

You are blessed,
creator of these pebbles,
you give me refuge,
in the company of the magnificent Jadiyetu,
unerring at her pleasant gatherings,
and more beautiful
than any of these young women.

When my mother received her cousin's poem, she in turn responded with another poem to show how she felt.

امسوحل ماه زاحل   خالگ تشواش اللا اسب

ؤ ذاك الرك الساحل   افكدني بكد اوسرد

From the east,
I am overcome
by sweet anguish and sorrow,
and I remember
the hills of Auserd
when I look east, toward
that crystalline white quartz rock.

My mother's response with a poem about Tiris got my
sister Lehbeila involved, and she, too, composed another
poem as the preparations began for their return to the
refugee camps. She wanted to use her poem to bid farewell to those pleasant places and to highlight the qualities
of some family members with whom they had spent
those camping days.

اعلى الخير ؤ حسن الجور   الـڭلاب متلطما
و اسل الطش مشكور   يايوڭي بعد ابفاطم

I leave behind those hills
that close off their valleys after me,
preserving peace
and good neighborliness.
And I say,
"Beloved Fatma."
And I say,
"You are blessed, dear Tasha."

My mother was a well-known person who was mentioned by several poets during her lifetime. I have managed to compile some poems about her youth with the help of my sisters, Lehbeila, Nana, and Suadu, who live in the Saharawi refugee camps.

This poem was dedicated to my mother at the time when her family was traveling as nomads in an area very close to the Edejen pools, some sixty kilometers from the place where my parents met in the late 1950s. It is attributed to two of her male peers. In Saharawi society, anyone, especially poets, can compliment a woman on her qualities and her character without it being misconstrued.

بيه اجبر حد اڭديد	من لزم العڭل الي اتراد
ڭدو و ازوين اخديد	ازوين ردو و ازوين زاد

There is a reason why
my heart flutters.
It has found someone
who suits it perfectly,
who is witty in conversation,
who is slender in build, and
who has a beautiful face.

The other poems that I reproduce below are by Mohamed Moulud Uld Bah, alias Baduh. He was an exemplary poet who spent his itinerant life in Tiris and Zemur.

He used to compose in very intimate settings, inspired by his bohemian nomad instincts. He was born in 1879 and died in exile in 1976, in the Algerian city of Tindouf. He dedicated this *gaf*, or short poem, to my mother, Jadiyetu Omar, and to another woman, a friend of hers called Jadiyetu Mint Boia. According to our family records, during one of his journeys in the region of Tiris, Baduh came across the campsites of the two women's families, with whom he shared family ties, and camped with them for a few days. In this poem, he sings the praises of them both.

ولي ذاك اسمي منتو   خادیجتوات الحي

خادیجتو عمار ؤتو   خادیجتومنت ابي

To the two Jadiyetus,
from the nomad *frig,*
I render my gratitude.
Not just anyone simply
gives their daughter the name
Jadiyetu, daughter of Boia, or
Jadiyetu, daughter of Omar.

This poem, which is an excerpt from a *talaá*, or extended poem, was composed by Baduh, probably around 1969 in the region of Legrea in Tiris. Baduh had traveled to Mauritania in search of a *tasufra*, but as he was unable to buy one there, he returned to the Sahara. On his way, someone showed him where my mother's family's *frig* was, next to the *frig* of other families who were close relations. After enjoying a warm welcome, Baduh recounted the story of his unsuccessful journey in search of a *tasufra*. My mother, concerned, suggested to another woman in the family called Issa that the two of them make Baduh the leather *tasufra* that he desired. The story of that simple act of kindness to make the traveler's dream come true was the inspiration for this poem.

عنك لحكّلي للي ولدت   اميلمنين وْلعليات اثنتين

عن خوهم عاد ابتاسوفرتو   تاسوفرت ماه ابلاديين

سبكّت فيها خاديجتو   بسباق و اجلود ازينين

و العز لبطن غالمتو   خاديجتو راه لجات

اتجيب الخير و حافلتو

Send a message to the mother of Moilemnin,[ii]
and to the other two ladies,
that their brother now has his *tasufra*.
A debt-free *tasufra*,
first crafted by Jadiyetu,
with colors of many shades
and lovely leather.
The beautiful embroidery
on its belly is
the work of Issa.

When Jadiyetu acts,
she does so prudently,
brimming over with talent.

The poet refers to the gift as a "debt-free" *tasufra* because he had previously tried to obtain one from Mauritania through some family members, to whom he had suggested, unsuccessfully, that they borrow one while they tried to find the money for it. Hence his gratitude, expressed through a poem, for the gesture shown by Jadiyetu and her friends.

In this other poem, Baduh mentions Nisha's daughters, my aunts and my mother.

امنات النيش زينات   ازين الي مايحتاج التحفال

و اسقام النيش و اليعات   فيهم فات انگال

الي فات انگال

Nisha's daughters
are beauties.
Their beauty needs
no adornments.
And as for Nisha's love,
and her passion,
what had to be said about that
has already been said.

The next poem, in which my mother is mentioned, was composed in the colonial era by a Saharawi poet who had a close relationship with our family but who always wanted to remain anonymous. In the poem, a powerful image related to water is used as a literary device, and I have translated it using "to emanate" and "to exude." It alludes to very pure water that springs very slowly from within the depths of a well and does not overflow or gush out. The image is used to portray my mother's discreet nature and her exquisite manners.

ؤلاني داير تعويج   الحگّت الحاسي ماه جام

ماهي دون اخويديج   دون اخويديج و انفس

Arriving at the well,
it was emanating
crystalline water,
and its springs
were gently exuding
pure water.
I do not intend
to waste any time
in seeing Jueidiya[iii]
because my soul
only loves Jueidiya.

Jadiyetu's characteristic personality was evident in her day-to-day interactions with us when we were little. Her intelligent reactions, which were compassionate and, dare I say, visionary, were a reflection of the fine ancestral wisdom of Bedouin women, and they are illustrated by an incident that happened to me when I was a child. I write about that incident in my book *Tiris: Rutas literarias* (*Tiris: Literary Routes*; Mahmud Awah 124–25).

Together with some kids around my age, I used to tend our camels very close to our families' camping sites. Whenever we did that chore, we each took turns bringing a small pouch of tea leaves with us every day. As the camels were settling down to rest when the heat was at its peak, we would get together under the shade of an acacia and make ourselves some well-earned tea, which we would sometimes have with pieces of unleavened bread. One day, when it was my turn to bring the tea, I took about a kilo's worth of my mother's tea, without her knowledge, from a wooden box with Chinese lettering and sheet metal corners. It was green tea of the highest quality, so I spent the day liberally brewing tea with my friends.

However, when it came time to go back to our families with the camels, I didn't know what to do with the rest of the tea, and, not wanting my mother to find out and reprimand me, I looked for a shrub that could serve as a good landmark. Right below it, I dug a very deep hole; placed the thick plastic bag, which was inside a fabric pouch, in the hole; and covered it up underneath the shrub until it was well hidden. My mother didn't take those mischievous antics of mine seriously, and sometimes she would laugh a lot when I came clean and told her about my pranks. Later, at her gatherings during the tea ceremony, she would tell her sisters and some friends about them, and they would while away the time, amusing themselves with my funny little stories.

Now, back to the bag of tea that I hid under the shrub. A year later, my family, my aunts, and my uncles camped in the same area during the summer. The whole camp ran out of tea leaves when the men had embarked on a journey in my father's car to go shopping in the Mauritanian town of Zouérat and would not return for another three weeks. The consumption of this plant among Saharawis has progressively led over time to severe dependency and even to unimaginable consequences, such as aches and pains, teary eyes, despondency, and moodiness, when there is a shortage. And so it was that the first week that people went without tea at the camp, the earliest symptoms of withdrawal began to appear. People at the gatherings found the conversations at teatime to be very boring and uninspiring. They tried to substitute the tea with تزوكنيت *tazaucanit* and الزواي *zauaya*, which contain certain stimulants, but it wasn't the same.

Seeing the situation, I remembered the pouch that I had hidden under the shrub the year before, and without saying anything to my mother, I discreetly went off to look for it. I located the bush right away and began to dig until I got to the precious herb, which was in perfect condition, with the plastic bag intact and watertight against the rains. I felt very happy about my mischief from the previous year. I was going to surprise my mother and my aunts, who had gone for several days without drinking any tea, and give them back their usual cheerfulness while my father and uncles made their way back with their purchases. I grabbed the pouch and hid it under my clothes until I got to our *jaima*. I was hoping to find my mother by herself so that no one else would see me. I wanted it to be just her and no one else. I asked her, "Detu, will you reward me if I give you a pouch of good tea for you to give my aunts, my grandmother, and your friends a treat so that you are all cheerful again?"

My mother stared at me as she read what my eyes were telling her. She knew that there was some truth to what I was saying to her because she saw it in that little face that she knew better than anyone else. Laughing heartily, she lunged at me to see what I was hiding underneath my clothes as I held on to the pouch. She exclaimed, "God bless you! God bless you! Where did you find this?"

The moment she had the pouch in her hands, she opened it, smelled it, and knew right away that the tea was still very well preserved. It was particularly good-quality tea leaves of the "71" brand, which was very popular in the 1970s and highly valued by Saharawis and Mauritanians. I then told her the whole story about the pouch. She lit a fire, gathered up the coals, made some food, and called over my aunts, my grandmother, and her friends to enjoy the stimulating and much valued herb. When they got together, she shared what was left of the kilo of tea among the families. The story of "Bahia's tea" and how it appeared just at the right time was the sole topic of conversation until my father and my uncles returned from their journey.

My mother left us in the refugee camps where she had lived for twenty-seven years, exiled from her home and her land. She was still optimistic that she would soon return to the home and the land that was usurped from us by the Moroccan regime of Hassan II, with his ambitious and bellicose blind faith in a conquest that encompassed Colomb-Béchar, Mali, the Senegal River, and Al Andalus.

She departed without ever forgetting the repercussions of that horrific image of the Green March, which we Saharawis refer to as the "Black March." It was the prelude to her many years of sorrow in exile that began in the aftermath of our betrayal and abandonment by

Spain in 1975. The hordes of people from the North in meandering caravans of old Ford trucks formed the screen that concealed the tanks and the more than 150,000 soldiers—flying the flags of Henry Kissinger and Hassan II—who were sent to kill and to die for something that was never theirs.

Rest in peace, Mama. You will live in me forevermore, just as the land of Tiris, with its wonderful people, its *galaba*, its *uidian*, and its elegant camels and gazelles, stretching from the borders of Dallet Am to the confines of the Adrar Setuf basin, will forever live in you.

Notes

i. She is referring to her family's name, *Ahel* Embarek Fal, but she omits "Fal" to achieve rhyme and rhythm in the poem.

ii. My maternal grandmother's real name was Moilemnin, but everyone called her Nisha. Her mother, my great-grandmother, was called Badia.

iii. The pet name by which everyone knew my mother in her youth.

Works Cited

Mahmud Awah, Bahia. *Tiris: Rutas literarias.* Última Línea, 2016.

Said, Edward. *"Reflections on Exile" and Other Essays.* Harvard UP, 2000.

Glossary of Hassaniya Terms

Ahel: Family. It refers not only to children and parents but also to grandparents, uncles and aunts, cousins, and ancestors.

Alah yarhamha: May God keep her in His best place.

Am el guetma: The year of the windstorm.

Am Elhuyum: Name given by Saharawis to the year 1958. It was the year in which Operation Écouvillon was carried out by Spanish and French allied troops against bands of Moroccans who had infiltrated the Saharawi territory.

amshakab: Camel saddle for women. It is used as storage for food and utensils in the *jaima* when camping.

anish: Acacia flower.

araah: A traditional Saharawi game in which a man stands in the middle of a circle and uses his feet to defend against attacks by players outside the circle.

asckaf: A shrub found in the *badia* and consumed by camels. Rich in potassium and salt, it gives a characteristic flavor to the milk of camels that feed on it.

asuaka: Rumors and gossip.

azzal: A castrated saddle camel trained as a pack animal.

badia: Camping sites where there is often grazing for the livestock.

baraka: A scapular medal made by holy men and worn to ward off misfortune. It is made by copying Qur'anic verses onto a piece of paper, which is then folded into a small size and sheathed in leather, silver, or bronze. In this context, *baraka* refers to fortune or good luck.

barracado: A camel's position when it lies down for a rider to climb onto or dismount from the saddle. The word comes from the Hassaniya *barrak*, and it was adopted by Spanish people who lived in Western Sahara, especially soldiers.

barrak: The act of holding a camel down. It is done by the camel rider or the person holding the camel's reins.

dabus: A traditional Saharawi game played with two poles, in which two men compete by jumping over and striking the poles until one of the poles breaks or falls.

darraa: Traditional Saharawi clothing for men.

deyar: A person who tracks down missing camels.

deyarin: Plural of *deyar.*

edabaa: The desert hyena.

edhen: Liquid butter made from sheep or goat milk. It is highly sought-after in the Sahara.

elgoum: Buddies.

eljarrub: Acacia pods that are edible when dry. They also have medicinal properties.

emrakib: Camels that have been trained as pack animals.

ercaiz: Poles that are used to hold up a *jaima.*

errualla: An expedition undertaken in the desert on camelback to search for water, which is carried back in large leather containers.

Etal Beit Shar: A Saharawi aphorism that conveys whether or not relations with a neighboring country are good or bad. *Etal* means "North," and it refers to Morocco, which is situated north of Western Sahara. The entire aphorism means that the North is the home of evil.

frig: A group of nomadic families camping in their *jaimas* at a place with grazing for their herds and water for the community.

gaf: A short poem.

galaba: Plural of *galb*, which means both "heart" and "hill."

ghazi: A group of warriors engaged in anti-colonial or intertribal conflicts.

grara: An area with groves of acacia trees.

guetma: A windstorm that is very well known for its severe impact on the inhabitants of the desert.

houl: A musical genre that is sung in Western Sahara and Mauritania. It is known as Hassaniya music, in reference to the Saharawi and Mauritanian societies in which Hassaniya is spoken.

huar: A camel calf.

ibil: A herd of camels.

Ina lilahi: A religious expression that means "Oh my God."

irifi: A hot desert wind.

ishiguin: Depressions in rocks from which sand-filtered water can be collected.

jaima: A nomadic tent. It is the traditional dwelling of Saharawis.

jarrub: Acacia pods that are edible either green or dried.

jzama: Braided leather reins that are used to control a camel.

kisra: The unleavened bread eaten by nomads. It used to be baked in hot sand.

lajabar: News that circulates by word of mouth among nomads.

lefrig: The *frig*. The word for "group of *jaimas*" (*frig*) preceded by the definite article.

lemrah: The traces left by a family after several weeks of camping, such as livestock dung, remnants of campfires, acacia branches, the three stones that are used to support cooking pots over a fire, and the bones of the animals that were consumed.

lharca: Camel cavalry that was tasked with protecting the territorial borders in colonial Western Sahara.

ljruf: A suckling lamb.

louh: A small wooden board that is skillfully carved by artisans and used as an "exercise book" by children at the *badia*.

main atai: A set of utensils used to prepare tea. It is made up of a teapot, glasses, and a tray.

maktuba: What is written. Fate. The faithful believe that the course of one's life has all been preordained by God.

melhfa: A fine wrap worn by Saharawi women.

menhru: The south-facing slope of every hill.

mirhan: The places where the nomads would camp with their livestock during prosperous times.

mus bleida: A traditional knife used by nomads. Its handle is encased in two flat pieces of ivory.

rahla: A camel saddle for men. In the Sahara, it is made from a shrub called *ignin* and covered with camel skin.

sadga: A religious act of charity that is supposed to be performed discreetly.

sajar: One who helps with preparing tea. The helper attends to the stove for heating the tea during the three rounds of the tea ceremony. The helper takes on those duties so that the person brewing the tea does not have to get up or bother with other tasks.

sfara: A species of gazelles.

shaif: One who sees well.

shara: A shooting competition.

Shertat: A mythical character in the Saharawi oral tradition whose stories are used to criticize bad habits in society.

shluha: Berber tribes from Morocco and other North African countries. Saharawis often refer to Moroccans by that name.

shuail: Camels that have calved recently and that produce very rich and sweet milk.

smayem: The appearance of some constellations in the summer sky when the heat reaches its peak, inevitably claiming animal and human victims.

talaá: A long poem.

talha: Acacia.

tarf melhfa: The end of the *melhfa* that hangs loosely over a woman's shoulder. Since it trails behind, children often grab onto it to follow their mothers around.

tasufra: A leather bag that is skillfully handcrafted by great women artisans. It is used by male camel riders to carry their belongings on the backs of their camels. It is also a component of the camel rider's outfit, which is made up of a *rahla*, or saddle; a cushion; a leather cape; leather bridles; and leather ropes.

tazaucanit: A plant used by Saharawis to brew a type of herbal tea that has various properties. It is used when they run out of tea, since it is also a stimulant.

tebraa: A literary genre composed and sung exclusively by women at private gatherings among friends and in the absence of male figures. The genre focuses on women's personal desires and may deal with love, politics, or heroic deeds.

tezaya: A camel-skin bag in which women keep provisions.

uad: River.

uidian: Plural of *uad*.

um talbat: A traditional Saharawi game that consists of knocking down flat stones placed vertically by throwing a stone ball at them.

wilaya: Province.

ya marhba: Welcome.

Yemaa: Representatives of the Saharawi tribes in the Francoist legislative assembly during the colonial era.

zauaya: A red herbal tea brewed with the bark of a plant. It is a stimulant, and it also has therapeutic properties for the stomach.

zgarit: A ululation by Saharawi women to denote happiness, victory, emotion, good news, or praise.

zibda: Butter made from camel milk.

zriba: An enclosure built with acacia branches that is used as a kitchen at campsites. It also serves as a pen to protect livestock from wild animals at night.

About the Translator

Dorothy Odartey-Wellington is professor of Hispanic studies at the University of Guelph, where she was awarded a Research Leadership Chair in 2021. She is the editor of *Transafrohispanismos: Puentes culturales críticos entre África, Latinoamerica y España* (2018; *Trans-afrohispanisms: Critical Cultural Bridges between Africa, Latin America, and Spain*) and the author of *Contemporary Spanish Fiction: Generation X* (2008). She has also published numerous articles and chapters on Spanish and Afro-Hispanic literatures and cultures.